TABLE OF CONTENTS

Quantity sales special discounts are available on quantity purchases by corporations, associations, and others. For details, contact the publisher at the address above.

Orders by U.S. trade bookstores and wholesalers. Email info@BeyondPublishing.net

First Beyond Publishing soft cover edition May 2016
The Beyond Publishing Speakers Bureau can bring authors to your live event. For more information or to book an event contact the Beyond Publishing Speakers Bureau speak@BeyondPublishing.net

The Author can be reached directly at www.LinkWithAlex.com
Manufactured and printed in the United States of America distributed globally by Beyond Publishing partners
New York | Los Angeles | London | Sydney

10 9 8 7 6 5 4 3 2 1 Library of Congress applied

ISBN 978-1-947256-85-9

Dedication

This book is written in loving memory of my grandma Roxie. I was fortunate to spend her last 10 years on earth with her. She taught me so much about life, love, success, & the importance of chasing your dreams. Grandma, I know you're my guardian angel watching over me and I hope this book puts a smile on your face.

INTRODUCTION

What do you see when you look in the mirror? Do you see someone who has been beaten down their entire life? Do you see someone who has tried over and over again to make it, to win, and to become successful, yet never got that break? Someone who has worked incredibly hard for that promotion, but never landed it? Someone who's looking for that opportunity to have a serious breakthrough?

Do you hear those voices inside of your head telling you that you can't do it, that you're not good enough, that you're not smart enough, that you're not strong enough, and that you don't even deserve success? Are you sick and tired of being sick and tired? Are you fed up with being broke, busted, and disgusted? Have you had it with being a poor example for your children? Are you not doing what you truly love?

Enough is enough, I'm here to tell you that you don't have to listen to those negative voices from within yourself and others, the ones that are so loud that you can't hear that other little voice telling you that you can do it. You don't have to listen to negative people telling you that you can't accomplish your goals, dreams, and fulfill your life's purpose, just because they never did. The idea that you can't do it is BS—you have infinite potential and are God's highest form of creation and capable of doing anything you want and obtaining whatever desires and treasures you seek.

I wasn't always successful, I had to learn from successful people on how to win big. A wise man once told me, "Alex, you don't have to be smart to make a lot of money and acquire riches. You have to find someone who has what you want, and you must say what they say and do what they do, and, eventually, you'll get what they have, every single time."

I'm writing this book because I'm tired of watching good people—people who want to do great things, people that deserve to win and deserve success! They just aren't getting it done, they're coming up short, and they aren't winning big enough. I want to see these individuals who have unlimited potential and personal power take off like a rocket ship! Everyone can do it, they just don't know how to release their potential and watch it soar.

That's why I am here. Let me serve as your tour guide to success and your mentor to making the rest of your life the best of your life! I want you to listen to me and follow my lead, until you think I'm lying to you or don't know what I'm talking about it. I can show you how to position yourself for prosperity and give you proven guidelines which, when incorporated into your life, will put your first $1,000,000 easily within your reach.

Close your eyes and imagine your ideal life. Visually paint your future life inside of your head, and put yourself there right now. Take a deep breath in, relax your body, and let your imagination flow and run wild. What do you see? How does it make you feel? Imagine waking up in your dream home, next to your dream spouse. Its 11 AM on a beautiful Sunday morning, and you have just woken up.

As you walk around in the vision, take note of your surroundings.

- What does your bedroom look like?
- What type of clothes are in your closet?
- What types of automobiles are in your garage?
- How much money do you have in your bank account, what does your daily routine look like, and what type of impact are you having on the world?

> Whatever you're currently imagining is what will become your future, if you can follow a few key principles to achieving massive success. You must understand that your thoughts are real, that your vision for your future is also real, and, if you want that image of your dream life to become your reality, you must get to work now.

God wants you to become successful, to live an abundant lifestyle, and to have whatever your heart desires. You must understand and accept the fact that there is an abundance of money circulating all around you, and earning a lot of money and becoming successful is actually fairly simple.

I didn't say it would be easy to earn a lot of money; I said it would be simple to earn a lot of money. There are some principles that I will teach you, but it is up to you to want change in your life enough to implement them.

I will take you on the journey from where I began to where I am now. Along the way, I am going to share the principles that I used to go from a broke college student to earning $1,000,000 in under 3 years. Unlike other authors and trainers, I am not teaching on hypothetical information or myths—I have personally reaped the rewards of these ten principles. I don't have to wonder if these principles work, because I know they work. They worked for me, and they also can work for you.

Follow my lead and listen to me until you think I'm lying to you or don't know what I am talking about. We will take this journey together and place you in a position where $1,000,000 is easily within your reach.

Alex Morton Facebook post (sophomore year ASU)
December 9, 2010

I want SUNS season tickets by age 25, i gotta pick it up.
O yeah.. Floor Seats.............duhhhhh.

Alex Morton Facebook Post
December 10, 2010

Possibly packing up everything and driving to miami and getting my real estate license and going hard with stocks after graduating next spring.... anyone wanna join?

Alex Morton Facebook post (Jr year ASU- 9th month into new biz)
November 20, 2011

6 months from now I'll be bouncing from city to city, college to college, plane to plane, building an empire & giving kids an opportunity to control their destiny, achieve their dreams, and create whatever life they desire. #blessed

CHAPTER ONE

LET YOUR IMAGINATION RUN WILD

Do you remember what you wanted to be when you were a kid? You might have wanted to be an astronaut, a professional athlete, or even the President. As children, we have such vivid imaginations and get so excited about the visions we have for ourselves and for our future.

Do you remember the teacher asking you, "What do you want to be when you grow up?" I don't remember all of my first-grade classmates' responses, but I am positive that no one responded, "When I grow up, I want to be told when to show up, what to do, when to do it, when to eat lunch, how much money I'm allowed to earn, and when I can go pee."

Growing up we all had big goals, dreams, and aspirations. Somewhere along the way, someone told you to stop being unrealistic. Someone stole your dream. You let someone convince you that whatever you wanted to do with the one life you've got wasn't a good choice, wasn't a smart decision, was too risky, and wasn't attainable.

> *You must remember that we are all God's highest form of creation, and, as such, we are all capable of anything and everything. It is our God-given right to manifest our destiny and turn our wildest dreams into our everyday realities.*

There are musicians, artists, athletes, inventors, and visionaries of all kinds. There are people in our world who put their pants on the same way you do, have two arms and two legs just like you, and, for the most part, are average people who had above-average dreams and goals and experienced extraordinary results with their time here on Earth.

The Wright brothers took an idea and turned it into a "steel bird" that allows people travel all over the world and have total freedom to adventure out and see the entire planet. Steve Jobs decided he was going to make a phone so sexy and sleek that it would become a must-have that would completely revolutionize the communication industry, and the iPhone was born. Phil Knight, a college kid with no business experience whatsoever, went from eating $0.99 burritos every night to earning over $1,000,000 per year when he started Nike.

One must ask how is it that some people make it big, while others fail. What does the individual earning $500,000 a year do differently than the individual earning $50,000? They incorporate a few proven principles into their everyday lives, and I'll be the first to tell you, it all starts with a dream. Walt Disney said, "All our dreams can come true, if we have the courage to pursue them."

SMALL TOWN WITH BIG DREAMS

I grew up in a small town called Bexley, Ohio. There were two ice cream shops, two pizzerias, and a lot of big-hearted and kind people, but there were also a lot of small, color-inside-the-lines minds.

I never did well with authority—I just couldn't wrap my head around the idea of being told what to do and when to do it. The bell system irked me to no end. Day after day, I was reprimanded, "Alex, you're tardy, again, what is the problem, son? You damn well know at 7:40am every morning, the bell rings, and you're supposed to be in your seat, ready for class. You can't keep stumbling in here, causing a ruckus at 7:43." It blew my mind, even at 12 years old how monumentally important my teachers found these three minutes, and I didn't like it one little bit.

My loathing of taking marching orders and following the herd mentality seems to have originated somewhere around third grade. I decided that my teachers were not my mother, and I was not going to let them control me. Throughout grade school and well into my high school years, I spent a fair amount of time in afterschool detentions and early-morning punishments.

I was always seemed to be deemed the loud mouth of my classes. I remember parent-teacher conferences during which the teachers would tell my parents, "Mr. and Mrs. Morton, it appears your son is always asking questions and engaging in classroom discussions, but he's hardly ever on-topic, and he usually makes a point to question all the lesson plans. He often asks, 'How in the world is any of this going to make me or anybody else any money?!'"

Even at 13 years old, I questioned the information that was being presented in the classroom. At 17, I began to argue about how they were trying to keep our thinking inside of a tiny box and punishing us for being too creative. Finally, at 18, I began to ask myself and then eventually them, "Who the heck do these people think they are, telling us how we ought to think, act, and go about life, and label us smart or stupid based off one damn exam?"

As a young boy, I knew that there were people who were living lavish lifestyles, traveling all over the world, making big things happen, becoming known and famous, and earning lots of money. From that point on, I began to seek out information on why successful people were successful and why others were not.

I vividly remember my high school's "Senior Day". We had an assembly during which all of the seniors in the school came together to discuss our future plans with the rest of the class. One by one, we each answered two questions: which college we would be attending in the fall and what we planned on majoring in.

A lot of the seniors who graduated with me were of high intellect and were attending universities such as Ohio State, Indiana, Stanford, and NYU. My high school was one of the top public high schools in the nation. I applied to Indiana University, Oklahoma University, and Arizona State University. Indiana rejected me, Oklahoma wait-listed me, and Arizona State accepted me. Back then, the joke was that if you had a heartbeat and could breathe, Arizona State would let you in. Apparently, I was deemed capable of both of those things, so I made plans to move west for college.

It was finally my turn. The teacher called out, "Alex Morton, you're up next."

I stood up and said, "Next year, I will be attending Arizona State University and I will be majoring in becoming a millionaire." The whole place erupted like a bomb had just been ignited. My classmates laughed hysterically and told me that I was "literally insane", "nuts", and "definitely not smart enough to ever make a million dollars".

I didn't feel embarrassed or demotivated. In fact, I instinctively knew, without a doubt, that I would make it happen.

That day has stuck with me forever. You don't have to know how you're going to do something; you just have to know that you will do it. Resolve to do the things that you say you are going to do, and become dead-set on achieving your goals. In order to succeed, you must know with 100 percent confidence and conviction that your dreams are possible and that you will stop at nothing until your dreams become your realities.

> *"First they ignore you, then they laugh at you, then they fight you, then you win."*
> *-Gandhi*

GET READY FOR BLASTOFF

Excitement and energy fuel the rocket, but a big dream points the rocket to its ultimate destination. It is very important to be excited and energetic about your future, but you must have a vivid, detailed, immensely scary big dream.

The mind cannot distinguish between fantasy and reality. You must plant the idea of your wildest and biggest dreams in your mind like you would plant a seed in a garden. Dreams work the same way seeds do: in order to prosper and grow, they must be cared for, watched over, protected, watered, and loved.

At a young age, I planted the idea that I would earn $1,000,000. I had no idea how I was going to do it—I just knew I was going to do it. Ask yourself who you are. What do you believe in? What do you want? What are you willing to do in order to get what you want? What is your life's purpose? It's okay if you cannot answer all of these questions yet, but I want you to expand your mind, let ideas start running wild, and start dreaming big dreams.

> *"Dream big dreams, small dreams have no magic."*

ANYTHING IS POSSIBLE WHEN YOU BELIEVE

A young guy named Diego had some serious magic and applied the dream-big principle directly into his life. One day, I received a call that someone from Cincinnati, Ohio had joined my business and there was something special about him. The first time I spoke to him on the phone, I immediately felt a connection—there was something magical about him. Even though I was in Arizona and he was in Ohio, I could literally sense his energy through the phone. I got on a plane the next day and flew to his family's home in the small Cincinnati suburb Mason.

At the time, Diego was living with his parents and brother. The entire family had emigrated from Guatemala. English was their second language, and at that juncture in time, they were enduring some serious financial hardships. His beautiful mother was cleaning houses for little pay, and his father was working at Subway—they worked hard, but they were barely making ends meet.

The first night I spent with Diego, he told me that he wanted to produce massive results in 2013. He said that he struggled through school, but that he had a burning desire for change and had always had big dreams from as early as he could remember. He told me, "Alex, I know where I am right now—where I am almost doesn't matter; it's all about where I am going." He went on to tell me his story, "Last winter, I rode my bicycle over two miles per day in below-freezing temperatures, ice, snow, and sleet, to work at a hotel. Once I got to the hotel, I cleaned the bathrooms, including all of the toilets. I tell you this, because I want you to know where I am starting from. I also want you to know that I have very big dreams. I see myself accomplishing all of my goals, helping my parents retire, and becoming self-made in America."

Diego went to work in 2013 and applied the principles I am teaching you in this book. In just one year, he went from earning $7 per hour to $100,000 in one year. On a stage at a convention, in front of 4,000 people, Diego was able to tell his mother that she could retire.

At this point, some people might be asking how that is possible. The first principle in this book is the principle of allowing yourself to dream big dreams and planting the seed in your mind that you will manifest your daydream into your reality. From there, it is necessary to apply the rest of these principles in this book, fueled by that dream and your unwavering commitment to it.

Diego proves that even if you are scrubbing toilets with a toothbrush, you can overcome any obstacles. If someone who comes from poverty can make his dreams happen in a new country, speaking a new language, you can do it, too!

It all starts with a dream—an idea of a better life, a better world, and a better you. You must understand that you have what it takes to win big in life.

> *It's already in you: you are a perfect, spiritual creation put on this earth with God-given talents and skills that you can utilize to achieve success. Plant that dream deep into your mind, water the seed of your dream every single day, by giving it love, attention, and focus, and your dream will become your life.*

MOTIVATIONAL MOMENT: I want you to repeat this quote five times before turning to the next chapter. Affirmations are very powerful and can bring you closer to achieving the life you were put on this earth to live. It will sound funny at first, but it works. I know it works, because I repeated it to myself every day on my journey to success.

> *"I AM GOING TO MAKE IT, I AM GOING TO DO WHAT IT TAKES TO GET THERE, I WILL NOT STOP AT ANYTHING OR ANYONE, I AM GOING TO BE A CHAMPION, AND THAT IS ALL THERE IS TO IT. PERIOD!"*

Alex Morton Facebook post
June 16, 2011

For those of you who promised me once I had my first $1000 month you'd take a look at my Opportunity... My phone better start ringing!!!

Marty W. to Alex Morton FB post
May 24, 2011

HUGE Congrats & Thanks to Alex Morton who Leaped all the way from Bronze to GOLD this MONTH! The incredible momentum that is catching the attention of top leadership would never have happened without Alex's vision & leadership.

CHAPTER 2

YOUR DREAMS START WITH YOUR WHY

Do you know your **WHY**? What is the purpose, cause, or belief that inspires you to do what you do? Take a moment and really dig deep down to the core of your soul and think about why you do what you do.

You bought this book because you had a burning fire within yourself to better your life. You want more out of life; you just need some direction on how to change your life immediately, make a complete 180, and start winning big. I remember the very moment I discovered my **WHY**, my reason to work diligently, my belief that inspired me to take all-out, massive action.

Once I discovered my WHY, that's when I became hungry—I mean really hungry—for success. When I was 16, it occurred to me that I was going to need to accomplish big things in order to feel completely fulfilled with my life.

My parents had set a good example for me—they really chased their dreams and made an impact on others. They earned a lot of money, and, more importantly, helped a lot of people.

My father was a college dropout turned millionaire in the insurance industry, and my mother helped run multi-million dollar businesses. As a teenager, I attended several of their company conferences. Each time that I attended one, countless people I did not know came up to me and told me what great parents I had, how they had saved their lives, how they had helped them become financially free and develop freedom with their time, and that my parents were "the real deal".

While it was flattering to hear these wonderful things about my parents, it was overwhelming, and, eventually, it started to mess with my head. I thought, "Holy crap! My parents are big-time winners, and I really need to figure out a way to make them proud. I am going to have some big expectations to live up to and big shoes to fill." I wasn't making the dean's list in school, I had no desire to become a doctor or lawyer, and I was pretty much at a loss as to what I truly wanted to do with my life.

If you are reading this book and still don't know what you want to do with your life, that's okay. What I want you to do is to think about what gets you inspired and motivated. What lights your fire, catalyzes important decisions, and causes to you to just go for it?

I realized that my **WHY** was to make my parents proud and prove to myself I was capable of becoming someone of value and making a difference, as they had done. As you read the rest of this chapter, I will give you a few examples of how this principle is extremely important on your rise to the top. I want you to think about your **WHY**.

What is going to cause you to wake up early and stay up late? What is going to cause you to put down the magazines, turn off the TV, stop partying, and start getting your life and universe ready to accept the massive amounts of goodness coming your way? Your journey to success and earning over $1,000,000 won't be easy—in fact, there are times that it will be very difficult. There will be times when you feel like giving up, when you feel like giving in, when you want to quit, and that's why this principle of starting with **WHY** is so darn important for you to reach your pinnacle of success.

Anyone can learn how to do something, but most don't understand why they need to do it. You must always start with **WHY**. I want you to find and discover your deep, emotional **WHY**.

One of my mentors told me, "Alex, I want you to find a **WHY** that makes you cry—make it emotional; make it meaningful; make it so important that it sends chills down your spine just thinking about it." If you can develop a strong **WHY**, you can truly overcome any obstacle, any objection, and any setback on your journey to the top. Remember, I want you to listen to me on these principles until you think I am lying to you or don't know what I am talking about.

I had no real business experience, I didn't have a big network, and I had no major skills, yet I went from earning little money to earning over $1,000,000 during the next two years. That quantum leap all started with my **WHY**.

PIZZA BOY TO $500,000

If I told you that one of my best friends, who absolutely had no God-given business talent, went from delivering pizzas on the weekends and bussing tables during the week to earning $500,000 in less than two years by applying the "Start With **WHY**" principle, would you believe me? Josh, who remains one of my best friends and business partners to this day, did exactly that.

We got involved in a business together, and although I took off like a rocket ship, Josh moved along sluggishly at the beginning. Keep in mind that Josh is a very smart guy who was studying supply chain management at a top 25 business school. He comes from a great family, and is an overall solid and genuine individual.

He was a normal kid, playing it safe, staying between the lines. At the time, he seemed content with working 40 hours a week for 40 years of his life and attempting to try and retire off 40 percent of his income.

I will never forget the day my cell phone rang on that hot, sticky summer day in Arizona. It was 2 PM, and I was driving home from a meeting.

Josh's voice came through the receiver quite monotone—he sounded afraid. "Alex," he told me, "my dad has worked for Intel for over 20 years, he's never been late a day in his life, has been a top producer his entire career, and, this morning, his boss walked in and notified him that he was going to be let go." My heart sank, and I lost my breath—I knew that this could be Josh's breaking point. Josh's father had a family of five, a big home in Oregon, two kids in college, and bills out the ears.

Josh interrupted my thoughts, " I'm now ready to build this business and go 110 percent. I need to make sure my family remains financially secure, and it's time for me to step up as a man and help my father through this tough time." He made the decision that same day to learn new skills, seek out mentors who could help him reach his goals, and made the commitment to earn a hell of a lot more money than delivering pizzas.

All of a sudden, Josh had no more fear, worry, or doubt. Instead, he was fired up and excited about his future. He had found his **WHY**.

He didn't know what he was doing and really didn't even know how the heck he was going to do it, but he knew he was going to do it. When you develop a strong, emotional, deep-rooted **WHY**, you don't have to know how you're going to do it, you just have to know that you will do it, no matter what.

If you lack that burning desire to chase your dreams and goals, you must find your **WHY**. People will do many things for money, cars, clothes, and other material goods, but the problem is that when they have a setback or something bad happens or their close friends and family are negative, most people give up, give in, and, eventually, quit. Contrast that with someone who has a burning desire to succeed, an all-consuming reason why they're doing something, a real reason to sacrifice sleep, to miss some birthdays, and to do whatever it takes to get the job done.

Now, instead of just working to earn money, Josh was working to save his family. In four months, he went from earning $1,000 per month to earning $5,000 per month.

Soon, he began earning $10,000 per month. Josh was scrubbing dishes and delivering pizzas and couldn't seem to get his business off the ground for months, and, then, he discovered his **WHY**, and boom, he takes off like a bat out of hell.

People will always do more and become more when they have an emotional connection to why they're completing the task at hand. What's your **WHY**? Is it to retire your mom and dad who have been working their entire lives? Do you have an enormous amount of student loan debt that you need to pay off? Are you wanting to fund mission trips around the world or feed the hungry?

Whatever vehicle you are using for wealth creation, whether it be insurance, real estate, network marketing, consulting, or medicine, you must have a deep, emotional WHY to keep you going through the tough times and eventually get you on top of that mountain.

CHASE YOUR PURPOSE, NOT YOUR CHECK

It can be very uncomfortable to admit that we are living a life that is not aligned with our true purpose, passion, calling, or most meaningful desire. Earlier, I mentioned that you must find a **WHY** to make you cry and really have a reason—one that you keep deep in your heart and soul to go after your dreams and goals. This book's main purpose is to teach you the 10 principles that I applied in my life to go from somebody with a big ego and a small bank account to earning over $1,600,000 in a blink of an eye.

PURPOSE is the key word of this section. You see, your **WHY** is the reason why you do what you do. However, your **PURPOSE** and true calling is the reason you're on earth.

We are going to get deep here for a second. I want you to imagine that you are lying on your deathbed, all of your family and loved ones are surrounding you, your life is coming to an end, and you have finally taken your last breathe. One, five, or ten years from that moment, when someone—perhaps a younger family member who doesn't remember you or didn't get to meet you—asks what your legacy is, what is it?

If you stay in the career path that you are currently in for the rest of your life, what will your legacy be? I ask you this question, because your true calling and your life's purpose may not be completed if you stay where you are, in your current job, in your current situation. It all changed for me once again when I found out my true calling was to inspire people. When I began to have success in my business, I began to inspire complete strangers, all over the world.

I remember traveling to 35 states and over 12 countries building my business, and strangers came up to me and told me that I had changed their lives—I had impacted and emotionally moved them and inspired them to take action in pursuing their goals and dreams. No matter how much money I made, nothing came close to feeling as good as hearing that from people. In 2013, I was 24 years old, and, in one month, I made $107,000, but the feeling of having someone tell me that I changed their life felt 100 times better.

I wasn't chasing my check, I was chasing my purpose. I learned that money follows meaning. I was living a meaningful life, helping and inspiring others, and the Universe was handsomely rewarding me for it. If you merely focus on how you're going to earn the $1,000,000, it won't happen.

> *You must focus on your true calling and life's purpose.*

A wise man once said that if you help enough people get what they want, you will get **everything** that you want. Take a second and ask yourself what were you put on Earth to do.

What are you good at? What are your strengths? Are you a great communicator? Are you good with technology? Can you speak multiple languages? What makes you unique?

Remember, money is just paper with ink, therefore, we should not focus on the dollar amounts; we should focus on impacting others. If you own your own business, what problem is your product or service solving? If you're a medical doctor, how many lives are you assisting to be healthy and well? If you're an attorney, how many people are you helping shine light on the truth?

One must focus on their true calling and purpose. Steve Jobs once said, "If you love what you do, you'll never work a day in your life." Is achieving success hard? Of course. No matter what you do, you will be working your ass off, waking up early, staying up late, and making sacrifices, but it's always worth it in the end.

> *Defining your WHY and starting your path to your first $1,000,000 with your WHY will give you new meaning to doing what you do, enabling you to do it with excitement and passion.*

Following your heart, discovering your true calling, and finding your life's purpose are essential to not only earning over $1,000,000, but to living a fulfilling life.

What is your **WHY** and what is YOUR life's **PURPOSE**?

Your WHY= making my mom proud & live Free life
Your PURPOSE= inspiring and motivate people For success.

Alex Morton Facebook post
May 11, 2011

Thanks for giving me 7 drinking/partying citations & kicking me out of the dorms freshman year. Thanks for the MIC & suspending me for a semester/putting me on probation until I graduate sophomore year. And thank you ASU for kissing my A$$ because I'm officially a senior and on track to graduate in 4 years.

Alex Morton Facebook post
September 28,2012

"If tomorrow wasn't promised - what would you give for today? Forget everything else. What would you think about? We get one opportunity in life. One chance at life. To do whatever you're going to do.

To lay your foundation and to make whatever mark you're going to make. Whatever legacy you're going to leave. Leave your legacy. Effort is between you and you. Effort ain't got nothing to do with nobody else. I'm pissed off for greatness. Because if you ain't pissed off for greatness that means you're okay with being mediocre."
#YPR #RightNow
#Ray Lewis

CHAPTER 3

RUN AWAY FROM THE 97%

Let me start this chapter by saying this: I do not know everything, but what I have figured out in my 25 years on this planet is that most people have no idea what they are talking about when it comes to living a fulfilling life, obtaining success on all levels, and making a "boatload" of money. Who taught you how to become successful and earn money? Do your parents truly understand how to become financially independent? Statistics indicated that they don't, unless, of course, they are in the 3 percent of people who earn the kind of money that you are chasing.

I don't mean to sound cocky, arrogant, or egotistical—my only goal here is to shed some light on all the bullshit we've been fed our entire lives. You and I have been taught to go to high school get good grades, go to college and get more good grades, graduate, apply for a job, and then go be told what to wear, what to do, when to show up, when to eat lunch, when to pee, and when to go home. And another human being is going to tell you how much you're worth by putting you on a salary or, even worse, paying you by the hour.

I am not trying to disrespect people who are earning "an honest living"—an expression I've never liked, since the majority of independent people are earning their livings honestly. I respect the 9-to-5 grind, and I respect mothers and fathers who are working three jobs to feed their kids and pay their bills; however, I am telling you that there are other ways to earn money, ways that don't involve you being a paid slave for the rest of your life and working a **J.O.B.**, which stands for **Journey of the Broke**.

I know some of you are saying to yourself, "this kid is an asshole, who the hell does he think he is, he's out of his mind." The reason I am laying it all out right now is because I don't want you to be stuck in a prison with no bars for the rest of your life and then get buried with unfulfilled dreams, goals, and ideas. We have a very limited time on Earth, and if you're not using it to become part of the 3 percent, you are living with the 97 percent of people who will never get paid as much as they deserve, nor will they ever have the independence that they deserve.

Think about it. Who makes all the money in the world? People who are entrepreneurs, people who own their own business. I saw a quote one day when I was a kid, and it stuck with me ever since, "If you don't chase your own dreams, you'll be hired by someone who did." For me, that quote said it all.

RUN AWAY FROM THE 97% means this: if the majority of people are doing something, reading something, eating something, drinking something, or thinking a certain way, you should, most likely, do the complete opposite. Growing up in Smalltown, USA, my out-of-the-box thinking wasn't always accepted. The teachers were always sending me into the hallway for asking questions like, "In what profession will I ever use calculus, and how is this going to make me any money to feed my future family?" The 97 percent don't like being challenged.

In Chemistry, I asked my teacher what "the damn point" of memorizing the periodic table of elements was. I believe in school, and I believe in education, but it's like the Paul Simon song, "Kodachrome", says, "When I think back on all the crap I learned in high school, it's a wonder I can think at all." The teachers cram so much information down teenagers' throats, the kids stress out and memorize all of the information, take a test, and then forget all of it. For me, rote memorization does not do anything to serve students' long-term goals.

In my opinion, students would be better served by being taught things that they will use throughout their lives, like goal-setting, public speaking, the magic of thinking big, laws of success, and how to earn a residual income. The 3 percent, including Richard Branson, Mark Zuckerburg, Sean "P. Diddy" Combs, and the late Steve Jobs, all talk about following your heart, following your dreams, going for it in life, making it happen, thinking differently than others, and innovating and creating. Yet, all of our lives we've been taught to color inside of the lines, do what we are told, respect authority, follow the system, and be "normal". We have been messed up, screwed up, and poisoned by the thoughts and teachings of people who have not done for it themselves.

In this exercise, finish each of my sentences, and you will quickly see my point:

THE 97%'S "SECRETS TO SUCCESS"

If you ever want to be successful go to _____, so you can get a good _____, so you can graduate and get a good _____.
Watch out for those get rich quick _____.
On your way to success, make sure you play it _____.
Money can't buy _____.
Money doesn't grow on _____.
Good things comes to those who _____.
If it sounds too good to be true, it probably _____.
All rich people are going to _____.

> *Walk Away from the 97% and Join the 3%*

Most people have the same thought patterns, and the same ways of thinking, which result in the same ways of living—and they can't help it, because it is what they have been taught their entire lives. Most people's lives (the 97%) will begin and end the exact same way. That's all they know, because that's what their grandparents and what their parents did, so they'll be happy doing the exact same thing and living virtually the exact same life. I am in no way, shape, or form saying living a "normal" life is bad, because it most certainly isn't, I'm just saying living an extraordinary life requires breaking free from the pattern.

Do what you want, when you want, with whom you want, for as long as you want. In order to achieve massive results, you must understand how crucial this principle is. You must accept that money is all around us, that we live in a world of pure abundance, that there are people winning big all over the place, and that you must literally run away from the 97%.

> *FORMAL EDUCATION WILL MAKE YOU A LIVING,*
> *SELF-EDUCATION WILL MAKE YOU A FORTUNE.*

Most of us, including myself, were taught that once you graduate college and earn your degree, your education is done. If you want to eat, sleep, travel, and live like the majority of people on Earth, go ahead and stop learning and growing upon graduation, and you will most likely end up like everybody else. Most people go through life like robots, doing exactly what they're told to do.

In my life experiences, I have observed that most people who are living mediocre lives stopped studying, educating, and growing themselves in their early 20s. On the flipside, I have had the fortunate blessing to be able to surround myself with some pretty big movers and shakers, people who are currently winning big, and big-time CEOs. What I came to realize is that **ALL**, not just some, but **ALL**, of these individuals have been practicing the art of personal development for their entire lives. The reason for this is that all successful, wealthy people understand the importance of always improving and always getting better at their craft.

In my opinion, you're either growing or you're dying, and death is bad, so we should all focus on growth. I don't believe in perfection; I believe in bettering our best. Regardless of what vehicle or opportunity you're choosing to create wealth, you will most likely have to become a great communicator, fantastic speaker, master networker, and phenomenal leader.

Mastering all of these skillsets will require you educating yourself. You will need to read lots of books, listen to countless audios, and study dozens of videos. I believe that success leaves clues. If you want to be an outstanding basketball player, you should study Michael Jordan. If you want to be a great soccer player, study Cristiano Ronaldo. If you want to become freaking wealthy, study someone who is freaking wealthy.

I'm sick of everyone and their mother trying to overcomplicate success. Two times two is four; that is an absolute truth. Whether we are in China, Africa, Denmark, Croatia, or Las Vegas, two times two is four. Therefore, there must be a set of principles and laws of success out there in the Universe, and if one follows those principles and laws, success will become theirs over time.

Growing up, the only parts of school I enjoyed were gym class and lunch. I rarely ever completed the required readings. As I grew up and matured, I realized that education was what was going to separate me from the pack, but not in the way that we, as a society, have been taught to believe that it will. It wasn't formal education that made me who I am today; it was the hours and hours of self-education.

At 18, I discovered a man named Jim Rohn, and my life irrevocably changed. Jim was the mentors mentor, with a true heart of gold. He has helped millions of people become millionaires.

I began listening to his recordings and falling asleep listening to the sound of his voice each night. I remember different girls who would spend the night say, "Why in the world are we falling asleep to a grown man's voice? That is just weird!"

It might not have made much sense back then, but I knew that one day it would—boy was I ever right. After discovering Jim Rohn, I got turned on to people like Les Brown, Bob Proctor, and Tony Robbins. I became obsessed with learning as much as I possibly could about successful people. I decided that if I could figure out how and why they became so successful, I could do the exact same thing.

Personal development is crucial to our growth. Not just financially, but spiritually, mentally, and physically. I am a firm believer that in order to have massive results financially, we must be at spiritual peace as well.

ACTION PLAN

A few of my favorite personal development mentors are Bob Proctor, Tony Robbins, Les Brown, and Jim Rohn. Play their CDs in your car, listen to them while you're working out, devote 15 to 30 minutes to studying them each morning, and if you want to make your spouse wonder about you, fall asleep to them every night.

Alex Morton
September 29, 2012 • Chicago, IL •

Keep studying hard!! Nothing like $30,000-$60,000 a year, and a 9-5, being told when to pee and eat lunch. I'm thinking once we have 10 YPR's under 25 years old doing $100,000+ people will wake up.. Until then.. Happy Saturday & make sure you get that GPA up!! Your boss needs you to be smart so he can go to Aruba & golf while you're behind a desk!!

CHAPTER 4

SHOWING GRATITUDE AND
THE LAW OF ATTRACTION

"It is unfortunate but true that for many people, 'life' is something that is going to happen in the future. They are always looking forward to the arrival of that big event or that big day."

Personally, I view myself as a near-psychopath when it comes to always wanting to become more, do more, and have more. No matter what I accomplished last month or what goal I made a reality last year, I am always excited about the next obstacle to overcome, the next challenge to figure out, and the next mountain to climb. On my journey to becoming a millionaire, however, I learned that sometimes, we must take a step back, look at all the beautiful and wonderful things currently happening in our lives, be thankful, and show gratitude.

> *Gratitude, to me, is simply being thankful for what we currently have in our life.*

Sometimes, we get so caught up with taking daily, consistent, massive action towards our dreams and goals that we never take the time to be thankful for all of our life's current blessings. Life is happening now, and it's meant to be enjoyed.

At a seminar, I learned that every morning, we should take the time to get out a sheet of paper and write out five to ten things that we are grateful for. I call this the Be Grateful Journal. The things you list don't need to be important events, nor do they need to be material possessions—they can be simple as a warm towel or a cup of iced tea. I know this idea sounds funny—and maybe even a little weird—but it is a simple way to bring a great deal of happiness into your life.

The act of showing gratitude and mentally thinking about what we're grateful for puts us in a great place mentally and spiritually. I wouldn't personally consider myself extremely religious; however, I am very spiritual. Gratitude is one of the most powerful tools in the Universe, but it requires engagement to reap its full rewards. Gratitude is also very important in setting and reaching our goals, which I will talk about later in this chapter.

> *Gratitude serves as a switch to energize and ignite our dreams and desires. The more we're grateful for, the more the Universe wants to give us. Gratitude also helps our vision expand, and it allows us to dream even bigger than ever before.*

I have learned how gratitude will enhance our clarity. Whatever we focus on during the action of showing gratitude will help us prioritize which goals are really important to us and makes us feel good, so we know what to focus on. The best way to relieve feelings of being overwhelmed and stressed out is to focus on what makes you feel alive.

At this point, you're probably thinking, "Okay, I get it—be grateful, write down things that I'm grateful for every day, and this will help me figure out what makes me happy and what I truly want out of life." You're exactly right.

You bought this book because you want to know what I did, how I acted, what I thought about, and the changes I had to make to earn over $1,000,000. It is vital that you do not overlook this principle. Being grateful is a huge part of the formula, because it is a stepping stone on your journey to success.

If you are always going one million miles per minute, you can easily lose focus on what's truly important. Things like your close friends, family, and even your health may get pushed onto the backburner because of how focused and driven you are. From what I have witnessed and experienced, massive success involves pushing yourself to the limit, making huge sacrifices, and working your freaking ass off.

I highly advise you to show more gratitude in your everyday life. If someone has positively impacted you in your life, let them know and tell them thank you.

For example, last Thanksgiving, I sent five direct messages to different teachers and professors I've had over the years to whom I was grateful. It took me roughly 30 seconds per message, and it was one of the best feelings ever. Not only are you making someone's day—maybe even their entire year—but you're also showing gratitude and focusing on what makes you happy.

If you want to make a million bucks, give, show, and exemplify gratitude. It works; trust me.

There was a time that I got so caught up in my goals and dreams that I let a lot of the world's beauty and life experiences pass me by. Remember, you can either learn by your mistakes or learn from your mentors. Hopefully, by now, you consider me one of your mentors—learn from my mistakes, instead of having to make the same mistake, yourself.

A few months ago, I embarked on an 8-10, don't quite remember how many, European countries tour. I traveled to Austria, the Czech Republic, France, Norway, England, the Netherlands, Belgium, Portugal, and maybe a few others to build my business and also to "see the sights". Most would agree that being able to travel to 8+ countries at 24 years old is not just pretty cool—it's a once-in-a-lifetime opportunity.

I had a great tour. I had the amazing opportunity to speak on stage in front of 4,000 people in Vienna, Austria, got to enjoy a lot of good food, and met some great people. However, I was so overly focused and engulfed in "pushing volume" and "breaking records" that I never took much time to sit back and smell the proverbial roses. I didn't go on any tours, I didn't visit many of the famous cathedrals, and I rarely took the time to even take any pictures.

While having "tunnel vision" when you are taking massive actions towards your dreams and goals can be a good thing, don't do it at the expense of taking in the sights, sounds, and culture of places most only dream about visiting.

Looking back on that magnificent trip, I should have stopped—even for just one hour in each country—to really soak it all in. I have had the fortunate opportunity to meet and converse with many millionaires—and even a billionaire—and they all agree that the road to success is even better than when you get there. Whatever your definition of success is, whatever your pinnacle level of achievement is, you will look back and remember all the fond memories, relationships, and experience you had on your pathway to massive success.

This story's principle is one that can be applied to anyone, anytime, anywhere. If you're reading this book and you have a child or children, spend time building those relationships and bonds that will last forever. If you have a loving partner, take the time to be grateful for having them in your life, make them feel special and important, and thank them for supporting you on your quest to having it all.

THOUGHTS ARE REAL

Have you ever wondered why some people are always struggling, in a world of hurt, suffering, and depression, living paycheck to paycheck and never making ends meet, while others seem to always get lucky and are consistently happy, healthy, and wealthy? What we, as humans, think about comes about and our thoughts are real.

I used to think that the idea that thoughts were real was all hocus pocus, until I found out that the majority of ultra-successful people use the law of attraction to win big in their careers and in life. We all must understand that we are living, breathing creatures, capable of anything and everything. We have the ability to control who comes into our life, what happens to us in our lives, and the ability to achieve massive success properly, using the law of attraction. People like Henry Ford, the Wright Brothers, the Firestone family, Muhammad Ali, Arnold Schwarzenegger, Will Smith, and Oprah are all giving credit to the law of attraction for their major successes.

One of my mentors, Bob Proctor, says, "This law clearly states you can only attract to you that which is in harmony with you. Everything in the Universe vibrates, including your mind and body. Look at your body through a microscope. It is a mass of energy—moving, vibrating. Your mind controls the vibration you are in at any given moment. You control your mind by the thoughts you choose. No one can cause you to think something you don't want to think. This is where freedom comes in. This is also where the problem begins with most people. They permit what is happening around them to determine how they think. 90 percent of the population wish positive, but think negative. Their negative thoughts put them in a negative vibration which, by law, determines what is attracted into their lives. As a creative individual, you will continually attract good things into your life by thinking positive thoughts and expecting the best life has to offer. You deserve it."

I used the law of attraction to assist me in building my business to 50 states—plus the District of Columbia and Puerto Rico—and over 53 countries. No matter where you are right now, regardless of your current situation or income, you must grasp this, because it can change your life in a blink of an eye.

How does a broke college kid at 21 with no background in business go from a bank balance that didn't even have a comma in it to $1,000,000 in a blink of an eye? I used the law of attraction to my advantage. Late at night, I would dream of and visualize myself as a millionaire. I painted such a vivid picture of what I wanted my life to be like that it was real to me. I would close my eyes and, in my vision, I would literally open the door to my dream home, drive my dream car, take care of my family, travel the world, and donate to charity.

Thoughts are real. When we think or visualize something, the Universe gets ahold of that thought or image and starts presenting you with opportunities to make that thought become a reality. When I scroll through old Facebook statuses, I have documentation of these visions—I began my journey by talking about traveling the world and earning a $1,000,000. Lo and behold, it happened. You can see this FB post on Page 8

Great athletes have known this secret for years. They see themselves winning the game or match long before they play the game. For the people in my business who are wishing for a new luxury car, I have them sit in my car, smell that leather, and grip that wheel, so that they have a clear picture—complete with all of the senses, except, perhaps, taste—to visualize their future and fuel their success.

> *You must understand that our minds don't understand the difference between fantasy and reality. We, as human beings, are God's highest form of creation and are capable of anything and everything.*

Exercise:

Close your eyes and really imagine your life as you would like it to be. Five years from now, where do you see yourself? Where are you living? What type of clothes are you wearing? What type of car are you driving? How much money are you earning? What kind of impact are you having on humanity?

When you visualize your future and go into deep thought, you are putting those thoughts and ideas out into the Universe. The Universe then responds, and you will begin to attract that future you see for yourself. Part of the reason why 3 percent of the population earn 97 percent of the money is because they are using the law of attraction to their advantage. Whether you believe in it or not, all that I ask is you try it out. Sit in peace and quiet for five to ten minutes and really think long and hard about your future, and you won't be disappointed. Do this DAILY for at least two weeks, and watch your life begin to change.

Alex Morton Facebook post
October 31, 2012 • Tempe, AZ •

Mark Zuckerberg, CEO of Facebook invited 5 people to his Harvard dorm room 9 years ago to discuss a business opportunity. 2 people showed up and joined him.

Dustin Moskovitz is now worth $6.5 Billion and Eduardo Saverin is worth $3.4 Billion."

The most expensive thing we can own is a closed mind! Thinking about "it" for too long can cost you a whole lot. NOW is the time to make your life become what you DREAM it to be.... tomorrow is not guaranteed, make today worth remembering... This IS the next FACEBOOK.. whether you want to believe it or not.. whether you want to accept it or not... whether you want to act like this isn't taking place in all 50 states.. whether you want to be a part of it or be a professional spectator... This is... ABOUT TO BE BIG!!!

RUN WITH IT.. OR RUN FROM IT!!!!
We cannot be stopped...
This is... A REVOLUTION!!!!! #YPR

CHAPTER 5

SETTING GOALS:
THE KEYS TO THE KINGDOM

Throughout this book we have already covered dreaming big, letting your imagination run wild, and finding a deep emotional reason why you do what you do. Now, we are going to take all of the information and tie it together with goals, or, as I like to call them, the keys to the kingdom.

> *"A goal is a dream with a deadline."*
> *-Napoleon Hill*

This quote by Napoleon Hill offers a phenomenal reminder to set some large, scary goals, get to work, and make it happen. Goals should be time-based, so that you have the drive to make your life better today, rather than putting it off until tomorrow.

Goals are critical to have any type of success in anything we do. It blows my mind whenever people set goals and then wonder why they aren't achieving them. Growing up, I thought setting goals was for the smart kids, the kids who were earning straight A's in all of their classes. Later in life, I found out that goal-setting is for everyone who wants to move ahead in life, get the job done, progress, evolve, and obtain success. Countless books have been written, hundreds of audio recordings have been produced, and thousands of videos have been shot, all centered around goal-setting and its paramount importance. At this point, we all realize that goal-setting is key ingredient to obtain the life we want, but, somehow, most people do not take the necessary time to thoroughly plan out an action plan, really develop a crystal-clear vision of what they want, and set specific goals.

Have you ever written your goals down? Do you have clear goals of what you want your day, week, month, or next five years to look like? If you have, then I commend you and I am proud of you. If you're like the majority of humans, you need some major help on the how and the why for executing your goals. If you had asked me during my high school years if goals were really necessary, I would have laughed in your face. However, after studying why some people have success and why others do not, I am here to tell you that goal-setting is extremely necessary if you're trying to win big in your life.

Let me give you an example: If you were to board a plane tomorrow morning and the pilot came on and said, "Good morning, ladies and gentleman, we are taking off right now. We have no idea where we are going or when we will be landing, but we will let you know when we get there." How many of you would want to be on that plane? Didn't think so. But that's exactly how most people go through life. They lollygag around, only put in half-ass effort, and give up and quit on something they truly desire. As sad as it is to say, most people never accomplish anything worthwhile. Most people stay in line, keep their mouths shut, follow all the rules, do what they're told, and, as a result, they tend to remain average and mediocre.

> *Setting goals is the best way to go from where you are to where you desire to be. It's critical to always begin with the end in mind.*

Earlier, I talked about seeing yourself in the future, driving your dream car, living in your dream home, and literally living your dream life. Goals are what will get you there. I know you have what it takes already deep inside of you to achieve greatness; this book will simply help you become aware of your potential and fire you up to go make it happen.

Moving forward, your goals should be focused around things that you have never done before, not repeating past success, or you will never reach new heights and experience the joy of achieving something greater than you've ever achieved before. Goals are designed to help you grow and forces you to bring out something from inside of you that you didn't even know was there in the first place. If you already know exactly how to accomplish your goal, it is not going to do what goals are designed to do. If you're really going to accomplish something major, it's going to need to inspire you to put in the necessary time, energy, and effort it's going to take to make it happen. The bottom line is that you must set a large, scary goal. If it doesn't scare the heck out of you, it is not big enough.

I am now going to dive into three types of goals one can set when looking to advance in their life. I refer to these three types of goals as A-type, B-type, and C-type goals.

Once you see all of this explained, you're going to think to yourself, "Wow, this is pretty amateur stuff—a fifth-grader could handle this." Let me let you in on a little secret: goal-setting is very elementary. I am a firm believer that small children could understand how to set goals, devise a plan, and accomplish what they set out to do if they were taught this at an early age.

A-TYPE GOALS

A. type goals are where most people live and never leave. An A-type goal is a goal that is based on your present results, which really doesn't constitute a goal at all. I would bet that the majority of people around you—your friends, your family, and your coworkers—are A-type goal people.

One time, I was in Orlando, speaking to a room full of people, and a young guy came up to me and asked me to go over his goals with him. He then told me his goal was to get a new BMW. I asked him what he was currently driving, and he told me that he was driving a five-year-old BMW and that he wanted a newer one. I looked at him and said, "You've known for five years how to get a new BMW, therefore, you're not stretching one bit, so this does not qualify as a goal."

It's very important that you understand that this is where people want you to be. Your friends—and even your family—like you with the A-type goal mindset. They don't want you to leave, so, if you ever set a goal that's out of this A-type region, they're probably not going to support you. It's not that they don't love you or that they don't want you to win—the truth is that they don't want you to leave.

There really isn't much to grasp, get, and grow over here in A-Type Land, so I would strongly suggest you get out of here and stop setting goals based on present results. An A-type goal is what you KNOW you can do.

B-TYPE GOALS

Once you decide to leave the world of A-type goals, you'll move onto the B-type. This is where some of the big shots, head honchos, and mover and shakers (or so they think), are currently stationed at.

People who set B-type goals pay attention to what's going on in their lives. They know exactly what they need to do to survive, they know exactly how much money they've got saved up, they've calculated out every little expense, and they are really focused on where they are, instead of where they're going.

B-type goal people always have to have a plan, Well if this happens, and that happens, and all these things happen, then I can do that! Is that really the right goal? I don't think so. You already see how it's going to happen, almost like an A-type goal, so you're not really stretching and going for it. And, your A-type goal buddies aren't going to support you, because accomplishing a B-type goal means you're leaving them.

A B-type goal is based solely on what you think you can do. There is absolutely no inspiration in a B-type goal. A B-type goal is what you plan to do. Could you live an "okay" life in the B-type goals world? Sure, I suppose. But, if you really want to experience a life filled with abundance and freedom, you need to progress beyond this place, trust me.

C-TYPE GOALS

Have you ever caught yourself daydreaming before? Sitting there, letting your imagination run wild, visualizing your dream home, dream car, the dream vacations you've always wanted to take, giving to your church or synagogue, and doing what you want to do, when you want to do it, with whomever you want to do it with? Do you catch yourself saying, If only we could do that, if only I could go there, if only, if only, if only....

The funny thing about dreaming is that you can wake up at any given moment and start chasing those dreams to turn them into realities. Close your eyes for a second and revisit your dream. Imagine your life as you would actually like it to be.

In order to set a C-type goal you must ask yourself what you really want. What do you really want? You might have never had someone ever ask you this question, but it is a very important one to answer. You need to decide what you really want.

If you go back study people who left their mark on history, they were, for the most part, average people with above-average dreams, goals, and desires. When you are living in the C-type world, that's where the magic can really happen. Forget logic, forget reasoning, and really go after what you want. Nothing wonderful comes from being logical and thinking small. The Wright Brothers, Beyonce, Bill Gates, Oprah, Steve Jobs, Taylor Swift, and Phil Knight all operated with a C-type goal mindset. Fall in love with your dreams and goals. Feel it in your heart, and get emotionally involved.

> *How does a kid who got kicked out of the dorms and business school when they were 21 make a million by his 25th birthday? It's because I am not afraid of losing, I didn't let logic stop me, and I created my own world and everything in it.*

You're probably thinking, Well, you're different than me. That's simply not true. We are both God's highest form of creation, capable of anything and everything we set our mind to. Live in the world of C-type goals—you'll learn to love it here!!

3 STEPS IN ACHIEVING EVERYTHING YOU WANT.

Fantasy, Theory, Fact.

These three words changed my life. Back at Arizona State University, I began fantasizing what my life could truly become, forming C-type goals. My imagination ran wild, and it became the only thing I could ever really focus on. I would close my eyes and see my future self, my future day-to-day activities, my future bank account, my future life, and my future world.

I want you to do the same. Close your eyes and imagine your life, designed by you. Once you get that image burned into your mind deeply enough and you focus on it long enough, I guarantee that you'll begin to turn that **FANTASY** into a **THEORY**.

Tell yourself, "I bet I can do what I want to do." I saw what I wanted, and, then, I saw that it was possible. I saw the $100,000 6-Series BMW in my mind, and, then, I saw how I could obtain it. I was turning my **FANTASY** into **THEORY**.

Lastly, you need to then turn your **THEORY** into **FACT**. You must understand that if you can see it in your mind, you can hold it in your hand. The Wright brothers from Dayton, Ohio were bicycle mechanics. They didn't know anything about flight, nor were they qualified to build an aircraft. They saw it in their mind **(FANTASY)**, they began believing it was possible **(THEORY)**, and, then, they opened up the kingdom of flight **(FACT)**.

> *This is major stuff. These three steps can and will change your life once you apply them. I saw the fantasy of what I wanted in my mind, found a way that would make it possible, and turned it into reality. You can do the same. If I can do it, so can you.*

WOULD YOU LIKE FRIES WITH THAT?

Let me give you a real-life example of the importance of setting C-type goals. Back in late 2011, I met a 17-year-old kid who was sign-spinning on the side of the highway in the hot Arizona summers and had a part-time job flipping burgers at McDonald's.

You're probably thinking to yourself that there is no way on God's green Earth that this kid "makes it". It doesn't get much worse than pouring sweat all day in the unrelenting, scorching sun and going home from work smelling of oil from the fryer.

One day, my friend, Andrew, called me and said, "I've got this young kid named Cody. He's actually still in high school, but he's very determined to become successful." I was thinking, I remember when I was in high school, and all I cared about was sports and girls. I also remembered that 17 was the age at which I really figured out that one day, I was going to make it big and earn lots of money. I told Andrew that if he truly believed in "this Cody kid", to send him over to my condo. A few days later, Cody knocked on the door, strolled into my condo, and we got to work. We discussed where he was at in life, what made him happy, what made him sad, and what excited him.

In the earlier chapters, we discussed how important it is to finding a deep and emotional WHY. Once I found out that Cody's main driving force was to get out of McDonald's, get a new car, and help his family out financially, that's when the importance of goal-setting came into play. I could have easily given Cody the same, tired advice that he had been getting all his life—to go out there and work really hard, and that, by doing so, all of his dreams would come true.

> *But instead of doing what most people do in business and sales, I decided to set some short and long-term goals with Cody. Using the C-type goal-setting mindset, we began to set specific goals, deadlines, and the mindset it was going to take to turn a sign-spinning burger-maker into a champion.*

I told Cody to let his imagination run wild and to really think about what he wanted. In the specific business we were building, he needed to set goals on becoming a better speaker, become a better presenter, and become a master at closing sales. He also set goals to increase his knowledge on the specific product line and demographic we were focusing on.

Cody began a pattern of setting and crushing goals. Set a goal, crush it. Set another goal, crush it. Cody became obsessed with success, focused, and he really poured his blood, sweat, and tears into his dream of becoming successful.

He set specific goals of the ranks in the company he wanted to hit. He made sure all of his goals were measurable, so he could track his progress and break what he needed to do to achieve his goals down into daily objectives. He began to realize that all of his goals were attainable, so he began to practice and possess the needed skills and attributes to turn his dreams into his reality.

Most of the goals he set were realistic. I am a firm believer that you should never be realistic. I don't think it was "realistic" for a McDonald's employee to earn his first $100K as a successful entrepreneur before he could legally drink alcohol, and I don't think it was "realistic" to think that I could ever earn $1,000,000, considering I was politely kicked out of my business school.

The word "realistic" here (specifically for Cody) was to figure out how much work, time, energy, effort it would take to accomplish a goal, and then set his goals according to his level of desire.

> No one is going to pay you professional income with an amateur work ethic.

Last but not least, we made sure that Cody was going to accomplish his goals in a timely manner. We set stepping stones, or progress points, along the way on his journey to a six-figure income. Without proper C-type goal-setting, it would have been very difficult for Cody to accomplish what he did. Similarly, it would be impossible for you to read this book, take action without setting goals, and achieve massive results.

To this very day, Cody and I are very good friends and, because this kid truly made such an impact on my life, I am going to share with you how he used visualization and the law of attraction to get his BMW dream car. When I met Cody, he was driving a beat-up, 2000 Jeep Cherokee. In my company, when someone hits a certain number of sales, they qualify for a car bonus. I told Cody to print off a picture of the exact car he desired, and to post that picture everywhere in his home. At first, Cody told me I was "straight crazy", but he listened to me, nonetheless. I remember going to his house, where he lived in his parents' basement, and seeing that BMW posted everywhere. On the refrigerator, above his bed, and even on the bathroom wall, Cody had plastered his dream of acquiring a white BMW 328i. His mom, Tina, asked me, "Alex, what in the hell are you doing to my son?"

I replied, "You will find out soon!"

It took Cody several months, but guess which car he picked up from the dealership? You're darn right! The white BMW 328i was in his driveway at the ripe old age of 18.

You see, these principles work. It's exactly what I—and so many people I helped—did to go from zero to hero in a blink of an eye.

Upon finishing this book, it will be your duty, responsibility, and obligation to follow the success principles we are discussing. When you do, your life will change forever, and you will begin to win big in all areas of your life.

CHALLENGE ACCEPTED

It was a normal afternoon at Arizona State University. I was sitting on my couch in my condo, planning out the week's events and figuring out which of my leaders I needed to focus on to help them achieve their monthly goals.

That's when the phone rang. One of my mentors, Brad, called me and said, "I was looking at your numbers for last month, and your team did about $12,000 in sales volume. Our company's convention is in four months, and, if you can go from $12,000 to $54,000 in monthly sales, I will let you speak on stage in front of 8,000 people. That's all. Good bye."

My jaw dropped to the floor. I was extremely excited, and, simultaneously, extremely scared. One of my biggest dreams was to speak on stage in front of thousands of people, and this was my first legitimate shot at turning that dream into a reality.

Knowing what I knew about goal-setting and beginning with the end in mind, I began to develop a four-month plan to more than double my sales organization. It was not "realistic" to double our team in such a short amount of time, and most of my leaders thought I was crazy. But, I already saw it in my head, so I knew that it was possible. I didn't know exactly how it was going to happen, but it was going to happen, and I was going to get my 21-year-old butt on that stage and light the world on fire.

I set daily, weekly, and monthly goals and became disgustingly obsessed with making this happen. You must become obsessed with what you want. Teachers, parents, or your spouse may tell you otherwise, but I don't care: if you want to make big strides in your life and make big bucks, you must become obsessed. Get obsessed enough that you will turn off the television, but pick up a book. Obsessed enough to turn off the radio, but play self-development tapes. You'll turn your mind into a success-attracting machine, and you will do whatever it takes to achieve your desired goals.

I became obsessed. My friends, family, and even some of my business partners told me my goal was too steep, too large, too scary, and there was a very small chance of me hitting my goal of more than doubling my organization in under four months. I began with the end in mind. I sacrificed some weekends when all my friends would go out and party, and I stayed in and studied the successful people who were winning big in my industry. I even told my girlfriend at the time that I could only see her from 12 AM until 2 AM on a nightly basis, because, outside of those hours, I was engaging in income-producing activities.

Month four came around, and my team didn't just do $54,000 in sales volume—we ended month four with $65,880 in total sales. I got to speak in front of 8,000 people at Caesar's Palace in Las Vegas that month, and I was so darn proud of myself that I could have cried.

You might be asking yourself what I did during those four months that I hadn't been doing prior. The product cost the same, we had the same CEO, and the compensation plan was the same, so what happened and what caused this enormous growth?

Goal-setting made it possible. When you set your mind to something, paint that vivid picture of what your truly want, and develop that action plan to reach your goal, it all becomes possible. Your confidence skyrockets, your conviction in meetings goes through the roof, and, most importantly, the people around you will catch your excitement, energy, and enthusiasm, and get lit on freaking fire. I call this phenomenon "the stars aligning in the Universe".

> *When you are focused, committed, and consistent in your daily actions and habits, you cannot lose.*

Whatever business you're involved in, whatever company you own, operate, or work for, understand this: goal-setting is paramount. Set big, scary, insane goals, make your action plan, live in the C-type world, and pursue them with relentless actions.

I do not care who you pray to, who your daddy is, nor do I care how much money you have—everyone can do it when they are equipped with the principles I used to obtain massive success. I want **YOU** to truly believe deep down that **YOU** deserve success, **YOU** desire success, and **YOU** will attract and acquire success. I believe in your dreams, and I believe in **YOU**.

When you set a goal, it's got to scare you. I want you to write out your goal in the present tense, starting with the phrase, "I am so happy and grateful now that..." Don't let your goals and dreams slip away from you. Claim them and make them happen! They're yours.

> *I want you to truly believe deep down that your deserve success, you desire success, and you will attract and acquire success. I believe in your dreams, and I believe in YOU!*

Now, go accomplish what you want, and make the rest of your life the best of your life.

SETTING GOALS ACTION PLAN

"We are at our very best, and we are happiest, when we are fully engaged in work we enjoy on the journey toward the goal we've established for ourselves. It gives meaning to our time off and comfort to our sleep. It makes everything else in life so wonderful, so worthwhile."

-Earl Nightingale

1. Get crystal-clear on where you want to be in three months. In six months. In nine months. In 12 months.
2. Determine your top three personal, health, and financial goals for the next 90 days.

Use reverse-engineering. You must begin with the end in mind.

---

1. Set your month one goal.
2. Set your month two goals.
3. Set your month three goals.
4. Drill down and establish your weekly action goals for each month, starting with your desired results.

Write these down on paper and read them each and every day. Read them when you wake up in the morning and when you go to sleep at night, so they are first thing and the last thing you think about for the day. FOCUS, FOCUS, FOCUS. You have to see these goals accomplished in your mind. Close your eyes. Visualize how you will feel when you have accomplished your plan. Go out and start achieving your goals.

Alex Morton
December 2, 2012 •

A lot of people say they want to be successful. But they would rather eat, sleep, & party more than they want success. Anyone who has ever achieved a high level of success has sacrificed many things to get to where they wanted to go. If you think the top #YPR leaders put ANYTHING in front of their business besides God & family you've lost your mind..

Work your ass off now, give up sleep now, skip meals now.. To get to where you want to go. WALK AWAY from the 97 percent! Don't say what they say! Don't do what they do! Don't have days like they have!!

We will have plenty of time to party & have fun on our jets, helicopters, & yachts in in later years.

Do what others won't today so you can live like others can't tomorrow. #YPR #GameTime
— at Phoenix Sky Harbor International Airport.

CHAPTER 6

GET LASER-FOCUSED

"FOCUS, Alex, FOCUS, Alex, FOCUS, Alex! It's only 135 pounds, dammit! FOCUS, Alex, FOCUS, FOCUS, FOCUS!", shouted the Bexley High School football strength and conditioning coach, Coach Knapp.

Good 'ole Coach Knapp was an impressive man. At 6'1" and 275 pounds, with a huge belly, burly beard, tattoos, and his tobacco-spitting, Harley Davidson-riding, don't-give-a-darn-if-you-live-or-die in the weight room attitude, he was one mean man.

There was nothing worse than lifting days with Coach Knapp. I was in the squat rack with 135 pounds resting on my neck, doing parallel squats. The 135 pounds wasn't the problem; it was the amount of repetitions I had to perform: "until you puke, faint, or die."

I will never forget that Saturday morning lift, during which I was the last player to go into the squat rack. I probably cranked out a solid 30 to 40 reps, which was good for me, considering that I was a 225-pounder who huffed down his mama's homemade food every night. It was me, the squat rack, and Coach Knapp. His cold eyes bore into my very soul as he shouted, "More, more, more! Give me one more, give me one more! You're tougher than that, you're better than that! FOCUS, FOCUS, FOCUS, FOCUS! I said FOCUS!" I did as many reps as I could before melting into the floor, certain of my imminent death.

I got laser-focused at the task at hand, and all I thought about was doing one more rep. In order to live a great life and win big in business, you must apply the same laser-focus to what you want and how you're going to get it.

> *Most dictionaries define focus as, "The ability to give all of your time, energy, and activity to a particular activity."*

Whether it's a sport, academics, or business, the ability to get focused is crucial for one's success. When you are able to focus, it lets you zero in on the specifics, keeps you crystal-clear on the task at hand, and helps you get things done with higher energy, a higher quality of work, and in a timely manner.

FOCUS ON YOUR STRENGTHS

This is a pretty simple concept here. We are all good at certain things and not-so-good at other things.

I want you to focus on your strengths. Take a second, sit back, take a deep breath in, and really think about what you're good at. Write down anything you consider yourself "better at than most people".

I did this exact exercise when I was 18 years old, sitting in the back of the Biology 101 classroom at Arizona State University. As usual, instead of paying attention to class, I was thinking about what I could do to start making money. I took out a piece of paper, and, at the top of it, I wrote "STRENGTHS" in big, bold capital letters.

While doing this exercise, it is also a good idea to jot down what you're not-so-good at. By taking note of your weaknesses, you can focus more on your strengths.

Under "STRENGTHS", I wrote: speaking, writing, finishing things on time, and persuading people to do what I want them to do. I even wrote down selling, despite the fact that I had never really sold anything before. At the end of the list, I added "girls", since I thought I was quite the ladies' man. On the other side of the paper—the areas where I lacked—I wrote: math, science, and anything that has to do with technology.

I also want you to think about things you're naturally good at. When someone is naturally good at something, they have a higher chance of becoming great over someone who has learned the skills to be good. Lebron James was naturally good at basketball; he discovered this, and became great. On the other hand, if you get so caught up with turning your weaknesses into your strengths, you could be wasting time, energy, and effort.

In the early stages of my career, I was told by my peers that I was a "pretty good, but not great" public speaker. I've always been a loudmouth, and in high school, I had been elected captain of my football team, because I could get the team fired up and excited through speech. Once I came to this realization, I began to study how to go from being a good speaker to a great one. I sat up late at night, watching YouTube videos of people like Martin Luther King, Barack Obama, Tony Robbins, and even memorable award show speeches. I told myself that if all of these people could become great speakers, so could I.

I paced around my condo, pretending my hairbrush was a microphone, envisioning myself giving talks to crowds of 10,000 people. I imagined the crowd going nuts as I walked on the stage, and I would practice my speech, my pitch, and my success story, over and over and over. The saying "practice makes perfect" is simply not true—there is no such thing as "perfect": we can always grow, evolve, and improve in whatever we are doing.

> *Practice will, however, always make permanent.*

Like riding a bike, once you learn a skill, you never forget. Focus on your strengths. Everyone is good at a few things.

> *Discover your talents, embrace your strengths, and make the most of what you've got.*

FOCUS ON TODAY

"Focus on today" is so much more than just a phrase: it is a mindset. A winning mindset. One of the biggest detriments to success I've seen with individuals is that they spend far too much time reminiscing about the past or attempting to mold the future.

> *We all must understand that the past is the past, the future is a mystery, and all we can control is right now.*

It doesn't matter whether yesterday was good or bad, hot or cold, pleasant or sad. It's over with; it's finished; it's completed; there is nothing you or I can do to go back and change it, so stop spending time and energy on it. Let's repeat that one more time, so we are crystal clear: you cannot change the past, and you cannot predict the future—don't get stuck on either of them, and give your undivided attention to the present, what is happening right now, at this very moment.

Many people like to talk about "the old days" or "the glory days". Yes, high school was a great experience. Yes, I have lots of college stories to tell. Yes, my grandmother's homemade Armenian food was to-die-for. I will not, however, spend my seconds, minutes, and hours talking about these things.

If someone tells you that college will be or was the best four years of your life, it means that your life is stuck in one place and never progresses. The idea of peaking in high school or college is depressing to me. It should your goal to improve your quality of life every single year. I had a great 2015, but it is my duty to have an even better 2016.

We, as humans, must always be growing ourselves, pushing ourselves to become more, and always try to get better at whatever it is we are doing. What are you doing today to build your business? What are you doing today for your health? What are you doing today for your relationships? What are you doing to get one step closer to turning your goals and dreams into realities? Focus on today; don't look too far into the distance, and never, ever, look back.

FOCUS ON WHATS IMPORTANT

Focus on your priorities. All wealthy, successful people plan their days out in specific detail, and they allow others to break their focus. We all have 24 hours in a day. Every person on the planet has the exact same seconds in their day as you and I do. You might be asking yourself how in the world your friend who always gets it done and wins seems to get ahead of the pack, with the same time that everyone else has. How do they always excel in all that they do? How do they always seem to do way more than everybody else?

The winners in your life—the movers and shakers and top producers in whatever industry you're in—all play by the same rules and follow the same laws of success. One of those happens to be time management and the execution of daily habits that eventually turn into rituals. Take out a piece of paper, and write out your yearly goal for this year. Draw a circle around it. Write down the numbers one through ten, and, next to each number, write down the most important things that you must do on a daily basis to make sure that big far away goal of yours gets accomplished. Focus on those ten things.

You can use the "10 Most Important" list for all areas you want to improve in your life, from business to finances to friendships to relationships. What do you need to do to accomplish your goals? What do you know you have to focus on to make it happen?

Set your daily agenda, calendar, or smartphone app to give you a play-by-play throughout your day. Waking up at a random time, going to sleep at a random time, and doing whatever the hell you want during the day is not going to bring you the massive success you desire. You are a fool if you don't think the successful people in your life focus on what's important, and, for the most part, that's all they freaking focus on, because that is what's important in the first place! Cut the crap, and focus on the things and activities that you know must get completed on a day-to-day basis for you to win!

We all have goals and dreams, and, at times, it can be difficult to stay focused to accomplish them. In order to earn over $1,000,000, I had to focus on my strengths, turn my good to great, master the art of focusing on the present and making the most out of every single day, and focusing on the things that were going to get me from where I was to where I wanted to be.

> *It worked for me, and it can work for you, I promise you.*

Alex Morton Facebook
December 26, 2013 • Henderson, NV •

Getting mentally, emotionally, physically, & spiritually ready for a HUGE 2014. It's doesn't matter what we did in 2013, it's over now, I patted myself on the back, you can go ahead & do the same.. All those long days, longer nights, early mornings, drives, flights, sacrifices, travels, meetings, calls... COOL.. We all worked hard, but not hard enough. We all worked smart, but not smart enough. I have my 2014 goals laid out. Do you? Going to break 100's of stories of young people helping them change their lives , writing a book, & most importantly.. MAKE A POSITIVE IMPACT ON THE WORLD & BUILD A LEGACY MY FAMILY CAN BE PROUD OF!!!!!
#2014 #BestYearYet #SetScaryGoals #YPR

CHAPTER 7

YOUNG PEOPLE REVOLUTION-MILLENNIALS HOW TO CAPTURE OUR ATTENTION AND BUSINESS: THE PERFECT STORM OF OPPORTUNITY

Let's face it: the economy is down, the job market is terrible, student loan debt is the number one debt in America, and all of the baby boomers are still working. The old way, the old system, the old ways of thinking and living life are simply outdated—it's not 1960 anymore!

I can't repeat it often enough: the idea of going to school to get good grades, then taking out massive loans to go to college to get more good grades, to graduate to a job where someone dictates everything from when you can pee to when you can take your family on vacation is literally insane. To make matters worse, you usually have to work 40 hours a week, for 40 years of your life, to then try and retire on 40 percent of your earned income. It sounds pretty foolish to me.

Here's a question for you to think about: when is the last time you went to a retirement party? Exactly my point here, people—the promise of retirement is a fallacy in the modern era. It's time to wake up, get fired up, and take control of your life!

There is a "Young People Revolution" (YPR) that has taken place in the world economy. It seems every company, every CEO, and everyone with a brain is trying to tap into and, ultimately, dominate this segment of the market. Everyone is focused on recruiting millennials, attracting millennials, and breaking into the millennial marketplace.

In 2015, the Millennial generation is projected to surpass the "biggest of all time"—the Baby Boomer generation—as the largest living generation. Yep, you heard it here first, the Millennials are surpassing the Baby Boomers! We Millennials are people aged 18-34. The Census Bureau projects that the Millennial population was 74.8 million in 2014. By 2015, the Millennial population will increase in size to 75.3 million, becoming the largest generational group alive. Once one gets the attention of this market, one not only wins, but dominates. What we are talking about here is a big deal. Pretty soon, Millennials are going to be running the entire world.

You may be wondering why you should go out there and try to attract young people into your business, why it's important, and how the hell you can even do it. I'm here to guide you through the strategy that it will take.

There are many "young people gurus" out there who speak on these topics, yet they're 40 years old. That's like me trying to explain to you what it feels like to be on your deathbed. I've never been on my deathbed, and don't intend to be on it anytime soon. I built my organization from 0 people to 15,000 people all over the world, and most of the people in my organization are Millennials. I'm about to give you all of my secrets.

Being one of the first people in a multibillion dollar industry to crack this younger market wide open, there have definitely been some perks, and there have also been some punishments. Starting out, I was attending Arizona State University—which has 81,000 students—and, being able to observe so many young people at once, I noticed that most of them disliked being told what to do, when to do it, when to be in class, when homework and exams were due, all of that nonsense. I remember sitting in Hayden Library "studying"—a.k.a. memorizing—some random stuff about rainforest biomes thinking to myself, "How on God's green earth is this information ever going to help me make money. It totally sucks that I am going to sit here for the next eight hours in order to simply memorize facts, vomit them all over the exam at 9 AM, and promptly forget them, just so I can pass the course."

Most of the time, when I watched people walking on campus, it looked like a scene out of a zombie apocalypse movie or mindless robots stumbling all over the place. I know some of you are thinking I'm an ass who hates school and dislikes college, so, naturally, that would be my perception. I have a degree, my little sister has a degree, and I support school. I'm also not down on jobs; I'm just up on opportunity.

There are thousands of college campuses with hundreds of thousands of college kids roaming all over them. Most have no idea why they're there, dislike class, and are looking for an opportunity. I saw an enormous need to fill—it is literally the perfect storm of opportunity. If you are reading this, and you're involved in business, you should be focusing a lot of your time, energy, effort, and money on capitalizing on this market.

Remember in business it is our goal to solve problems and fulfill people's needs.

It hit me, and it all made sense: I saw the opportunity that allowed me to become a millionaire. When things make sense, they make dollars, and a lot of them! I got very excited about what was possible.

My business started with a small group in my dorm room and turned into a phenomenon. I am going to explain to you what I did, how I did it, and how my experiences can help you blow up your business. The YPR is taking over the world—if and when you penetrate this market, you can go from zero to hero in a hurry.

HOW TO GET THE MILLENNIALS IN YOUR BUSINESS

We, the Millennials, are different types of people. We didn't really grow up playing tag or hide-and-seek. It was more like Nintendo 64 and Xbox. Because of technology, we are very different than the Baby Boomers and everyone else who came before us.

We like things simple, hassle-free, easy, and efficient. We get bored easy, we all basically have ADD, and we want freedom. We want complete financial and time freedom. I can't teach you chemistry, biology, or Japanese, but I can help you break into this market.

There are several things you must understand and master before you are going to successfully get "us" to pay attention:

Understand that when approaching or talking to Millennials, we would like you to be normal. Nobody likes being sold, especially us. If you come off crazy aggressive, we immediately turn off. Instead of shoving your product or service down our throats and trying to "close the deal", it's better to come off as a friend first, business associate second. The keyword here is "chill"— life isn't Boiler Room or Glengarry Glen Ross. Relax and create conversation. We want you to ask us questions. We love talking about ourselves. Get to know us. Any time that you have a conversation with a Millennial, your goal is to connect with them.

I think a good acronym for this is F.O.R.M = FAMILY, OCCUPATION, RECREATION, and MOTIVATION.

Get them to talk about themselves. Once you get good at prospecting and connecting with Millennials, within the first five to ten minutes of conversation, you should get your prospect talking about their family, what they do for work, what they do for fun, and what they are motivated by. When you talk to us, you must genuinely get interested in knowing about us—we can tell if you are faking it for a sale.

When I speak all over the world, I always talk about how everyone should always be asking great questions. In fact, I guarantee you are one question away from a major breakthrough in your business. Girls love to talk about themselves, guys love to talk about themselves, and Millennials really love to talk about themselves. So, you, being a professional business person, need to ask great questions to get us talking. If you can get a prospect talking enough about enough topics, you will find what I like to call the "hot button".

Let's say you're an affiliate with a company that has an insanely healthy energy drink, and you're getting compensated for the amount of sales volume that you and your team produce. Obviously, you want to prospect and, eventually, recruit people with big social networks— those people are the Millennials.

Practice by striking up a conversation with a barista the next time that you walk into Starbucks. Your goal is to build the relationship, gather the contact information, and set up the next exposure. It is not to slam, bam, thank you ma'am them into purchasing your healthy energy drinks and getting them excited about your business right off the bat.

We Millennials are visual people. If your end goal is to sell us anything, you should be utilizing visual tools to do so, for example, a great YouTube video, a vibrant brochure, or samples of your products.

As I began to figure this out, I filled a cooler with my company's products every time that I left the house. Wherever I went, I sampled out the products. Every time I walked, into a gym to workout, I had my company's ready-to-drink protein shake, chilled and ready-to-go. Whenever I go out with my friends, I always have some ice-cold energy drinks in my pockets. Walking into a club or bar with bulging pockets may seem a little odd to some, but if doing that over and over again paid you $1,000,000, would you do it? Thought so.

Millennials love to be around high-energy people and places. If you're recruiting Millennials into your organization, talk about the family atmosphere, high-energy culture, and positive, motivated people they will get to surround themselves with.

One of the biggest reasons why my team grew quickly to 15,000 people was that everyone loved the "campfire effect". Our company's conventions, events, and meetings were always focused on creating the most enjoyable atmosphere possible.

Smile. It sounds simple, but something as small as a smile can cause a huge emotional shift in another person. This one may sound quite funny to you, but I have struck up countless conversations that led to business relationships by simply smiling at people. Not too many people smile much anymore, so when you go out of your way to smile, people take notice!

Be willing to do whatever it takes. If that means prospecting on a college campus for four hours in the hot sun or hanging out in a Starbucks for an entire day to meet new people, you must always doing whatever it takes. I can give you story after story of activities I did to grow my business that I did not thoroughly enjoy. It's not going to be easy—nothing easy is ever worthwhile—but it will be worth it; I guarantee.

COMMANDMENTS FOR ATTRACTING MILLENNIALS

1. Don't be a creepy weirdo.
2. "Chill", and don't try to close on the first exposure.
3. Genuinely be interested in getting to know the person.

4. Strike up purposeful conversations.
5. Ask questions until you complete F.O.R.M.
6. Utilize tools as much as possible.
7. Discover WHY they would do what you want them to do.
8. SMILE.
9. Do whatever it takes.
10. MOPFI Make other people feel important, especially millennials.

We know the statistics, we know the Millennials are taking over, and we have a firm understanding now that if and when you figure this segment of the marketplace out, you will be able to have quantum leaps in your business. When looking at the above 10 "commandments", realize that they are golden nuggets that can literally change your entire business, and make sure that you start implementing them. Although they are extremely simple, when executed properly, they work extremely well.

THE GIRL AT THE SKATE SHOP

It was a warm day at Arizona State University when I walked into a skate shop on campus. I was about six months into my career, and I was earning roughly $1,500 a month. At 21, working for yourself and having fun, making an extra $1,500 a month was pretty cool. It was my first real taste of direct sales, and, as you can imagine, I was fired up.

I went shopping that day for a backpack, because I was accompanying the CEO of the company on a business trip to North Carolina that upcoming weekend, and I wanted something to hold my laptop and headphones. As I walk into the skate shop, I was immediately greeted by a loud, inviting voice shouting, "What's up, dude? Let me know if you need any help!"

I looked over and saw a cute girl standing behind the cash register and immediately thought, Wow, I definitely need to talk to her about my business. I began aimlessly stumbling around the store, checking out shoes, t-shirts, shorts, basically every item except for what I originally came in for: a backpack.

Five minutes later, the girl came up to me and asked, "What are you exactly looking for man?" I told her that I was looking for a backpack, and she took me over to where the backpacks were and started showing me my options. I was cool, calm, and collected as I began asking her questions about herself: what her major was in school and where she was from. Eventually, I asked her the question that really ignites emotion: if what she was doing was her passion.

She said no and told me she wanted to travel the world, make money, and help retire her dad. At this point, I had discovered that she was not passionate about working there and that she wanted to travel, make money, and help retire her dad. So, within eight minutes, I had discovered her "hot button".

After she helped me find a backpack, I gave her a cold sample of my product, and we exchanged numbers. The next day, I followed up with her (the fortune is in the follow up) and set up a time for the next exposure.

She blew me off for a week. Finally, she got back to me, and we met up again. I showed her a company video (tool), and she enrolled into my business.

Kailey, "the girl from the skate shop", wound up becoming the fastest female in the company to hit the $250,000 mark, and she was only 21 years old. Anyone can talk to people, build a relationship, sample out product, set an appointment, follow up, smile, be friendly, utilize a tool, and enroll them into their business.

Remember, practice doesn't make perfect, it makes permanent. It can be scary to talk to a complete stranger; it can be awkward when the person you're trying to engage with doesn't want to hear it; it can even be painful at times. When you are ready to give up, don't forget that every single person who has achieved a high level of success has gone through the ups and downs and trials and tribulations.

> *You can do it, you can make it, just keep on keeping on, and never ever give up!*

Alex Morton Facebook Post
December 8, 2014 • Toronto, Canada •

Just got called out in front of 100+ people by my mentor Bob Proctor to write & have my book published in the next 90 days. #ChallengeAccepted

CHAPTER 8

THE WEEKEND THAT CHANGED MY LIFE

It was sitting in my home on a warm morning in Las Vegas when my phone rang. It was the weekend that changed my life, and the memory is so imprinted in my mind that it feels like it was yesterday. The vibrating phone's screen read "Incoming Call: Bob Proctor."

MY MENTOR AND FRIEND, BOB PROCTOR

My mentor and good friend Bob Proctor is one of the greatest speakers in the world. In my opinion, there is no other one person on Earth who understands the human mind, and just what it takes to achieve a high level of success, as well as Bob does. For 40 years, Bob has focused his energy around helping people create lives of prosperity, rewarding relationships, and spiritual awareness.

He knows how to help people, no matter where they are at in their lives, because he, himself, comes from a life of want and limitation. In 1960, he was a high-school dropout with a resume of dead-end jobs and a future clouded in debt. Somewhere along the way, someone gave him a copy of Napoleon Hill's Think and Grow Rich, which planted the seed of hope in Bob's mind. He began to read the works of Earl Nightingale and other motivational gurus. In just a few months, Bob's life literally spun on a dime. In a year, he was making more than $100,000 and soon topped the $1 million mark.

Bob moved to Chicago to work for his real-life mentors, Earl Nightingale and Lloyd Conant. After rising to the position of vice president of sales at Nightingale-Conant, he established his own company, which specialized in teaching others everything that he had learned on his rise to success. Bob now travels the globe, teaching thousands of people how to believe in and act upon the greatness of their own minds.

THAT LIFE-CHANGING PHONE CALL

When the caller ID flashed Bob Proctor's name, I was in shock. I look up to him the way that an aspiring basketball player looks up to Michael Jordan. I quickly picked up the phone, and Bob and I began talking.

He told me about the most anticipated seminar he hosts each year in Toronto, called "The Matrixx". This event is reserved for individuals who are really trying to take their businesses, finances, relationships, and lives to the next level. The week-long seminar, which costs $15,000 per person, literally transforms people's lives.

I cleared my schedule and put it on the calendar that I was going to be at The Matrixx event in Toronto, come hell or high water. In the weeks leading up to the big event, I invested time in watching some of Bob's work on You Tube and reading his self-titled book, Bob Proctor. I felt as though he was speaking to me, reaching deep into my soul. I felt a connection with him I really couldn't put into words. I knew that he had knowledge that could greatly benefit me, and I determined that I would stop at nothing to attain it.

Finally, it was time to pack my bag full of winter clothing and head up to Toronto. Prior to the event, he had asked all the attendees to come with an open mind, open spirit, and a big goal for 2015. I arrived at the hotel, checked into my room, and waited patiently for the 7 AM wake up call. It felt like I was eight years old again in Orlando, Florida, waiting for the Disney World parks to open. I woke up that next morning and got ready to embark on a life-changing week.

I can honestly say that those five days in Toronto helped me become crystal-clear on what I wanted to accomplish and how I was going to make it happen—I even wrote the first two chapters of this book during the free time we had in Toronto. Bob made me stand up in front of a few hundred people and publicly challenged me to write a book. He knew, and I knew, that I had absolutely no idea how to write a book, but I made up my mind that day that I wasn't just going to write a book: I was going to produce a tool to help people win bigger than ever before and live an outstanding life.

In these next few sections, I am going to tell you the exact things that my mentor, Mr. Bob Proctor told me during those five days that changed the course of my life forever. I will refer to these subjects as "Golden Nuggets".

I am 100 percent certain that when applying these topics to your life, you will be able to turn your wildest dreams into your everyday realities. I am going to give you both the lessons and philosophies, plus, I'll help you develop the mindset that he helped me create for myself. With this mindset, you will become aware of how you, too, can create the life of your dreams.

Nugget #1- NEVER THINK BACKWARDS

I am a very transparent person. I do not lie, I do not overpromise and under-deliver, and I straight up don't bullshit people. After the first day's event at Bob's seminar, I walked straight up to him and asked for his opinion on some past events in my company. 2014 had been a learning year. My income stayed pretty consistent, but the company had made a few questionable decisions that caused some headaches in the field.

Bob looked me dead in the eyes and said, "I wouldn't know, because I do not think backwards." The second those words came pouring out of his month, it was an immediate lightbulb flashing like a fire truck's siren in my mind. He preceded to give me an explanation on his life-altering phrase. He said, "Alex, let me ask you a question. Do you think it's possible to go back in time to 7 AM, when you woke up, and change anything about that moment whatsoever?"

Bob continued, *"Of course not. Therefore, I do not let my mind think or go backwards, because I cannot control what already happened. If I hear about something bad happening in the world, I don't go turn on the news station and sit in front of the television. I feel bad, of course, but there's nothing I can do to fix the situation. I tend to spend the bulk of my time thinking forward and finding ways to grow every single day and become the best possible version of myself. "*

When I first started my business in 2011, it was hard for me to let go of some of my past mistakes that were mentally holding me back from reaching my full potential. I always passed the courses, I always made the team, but I never reached the distinguished honor roll in class or became all-state in a sport while in high school. My freshman year of college, I got in so much trouble that I was called "the worst resident to ever live in the dorms". During college, I had to change my major several times, because I couldn't grasp economics or lab sciences. All my life, I was told I was good, but never great. Past experiences can cause fear and worry in your mind, which is not a good thing, because the mind controls the body, and the body controls our actions.

When I was 21, I allowed my past mistakes and failures to hold me back from achieving a high level of success right out of the gate. Stop for a second and think about your past. Were there ever moments where you thought to yourself that you weren't good enough, smart enough, or worthy enough of achieving success?

Bob Proctor taught me was that we can never think backwards: it simply doesn't do us any good. Yes, it is okay to think back on fond memories of childhood or a loved one. For the most part, though, your time is better spent letting it go and spending your precious time planning, strategizing, analyzing, and, most importantly, taking action on bettering your future and turning your goals and dreams into realities.

Nugget #2- IF YOU CAN SEE IT IN YOUR MIND, YOU CAN HOLD IT IN YOUR HAND.

The idea that if you can see something in your mind, you can hold it in your hand is one of the most powerful things I was ever taught. My first exposure to this way of thinking came from my parents. I remember when I was a little kid, my mother always told me what I could be anything I wanted to be when I grew up. I vividly recall the quote "If you can dream it, you can do it" being talked about at the family dinner table. My father would frequently tell me, "You have to see it first: you have to see yourself with exactly what you want, before you can ever make it your reality."

I remember when I was trying to become a captain of the football team in high school. Everyone—myself included—knew that I was not one of the best players on the field. My mother advised me, "Act like you're already a captain, be vocal, be loud, be a leader, and FAKE IT TILL YOU MAKE IT. See yourself as a captain now, before you ever get elected." I was voted a captain senior year.

At 18, when I got licensed to be a realtor in Arizona, I had no idea what the hell I was doing. Being young is often a detriment as a realtor, because potential clients assume that you not only have no professional experience in buying a house, you also have no personal experience in selling a house. My father instructed me to carry myself like an expert. He told me that if I didn't know the answer, I should find a mentor to get the answer from. Most importantly, he urged, "Act like, dress like, and talk like an agent who has been selling homes for years." I focused on leasing condos, since the market was dead during those years, and, working part time, I made over $50,000, in spite of my age.

In early 2011, when I got my feet wet with network marketing, my mentors, coaches, parents said, "What you're doing and creating hasn't been done before. At this point, if you act confident enough and enthusiastic enough and paint a clear enough vision of the future for others, you just may be able to lead a movement of young people who want to change their lives." And that's exactly what happened.

If you're reading this, understand that your results will not come from mere intellect and knowing more information. Your conscious mind will not move you forward. It's all in your subconscious mind. If you want to argue this with me, go ahead, but there's too much proof. There's a reason why many "educated" people never accomplish anything of major consequence, and some of the wealthiest people you and I know don't even seem that smart. We shake our heads and wonder how they did it. What you need to say to yourself is, I need to find out exactly what he did, so I can do the same thing. You must burn the image of what you want your life to be like into your subconscious mind—your future car, your dream house, the partner of your dreams, your bank balance, great health, and time freedom.

> *You must understand that THOUGHTS are THINGS.*

If you don't understand the law of attraction and how it works, drop your calculus textbook and go pick up a real book and learn it. What we think about comes about. PERIOD. And what we focus on the most will become a reality.

I attribute every success and also every failure I've encountered in my 25 years to the laws of success. If you research most any respected leader, famous actor, accomplished musician, or outstanding athlete, you will find that most of them will discuss the Law of Attraction or its equivalent. They will talk about their subconscious mind, and how there are universal laws working for us or against us 24/7, whether we like it or not. You just have to learn how to tap into the source. And it all starts with your own thoughts.

> *"If you can see it in your mind, you can hold it in your hand."*

Nugget #3- THE LAW OF COMPENSATION AND COMMITMENT

The Law of Compensation states that "The amount of money you earn will always be in direct proportion to the need for what you do, your ability to do it, and the difficulty in replacing you." Since you are reading this book, I would surmise that you like the idea of having a lot of money and would like to earn it in the very near future.

When you follow the Law of Compensation, you must position yourself for prosperity. In other words, you must make sure you're in the correct industry and selling the right product. A product that people love, develop an emotional attachment to, and cannot live without. When I started my business, I knew that I had to be working with products that people would love day after day, month after month, and year after year.

Secondly, the Law of Compensation states that the marketplace will reward you in proportion to your ability to execute. This means that you must possess the skills required for massive success, and they must be learned, studied, implemented, and mastered. It's pretty much common sense to understand that if you want to earn a lot of money in any given field, you're going to need to master the skills it takes to close deals and make it happen. The Law of Compensation works every single time. No one is going to pay you professional money if you only possess amateur abilities.

You also want to strive to be "irreplaceable." You must separate yourself from the pack and become a leader. I've figured out how to do this, and it's very, very simple. Get yourself out there, let yourself be vulnerable, and always be leading by example. In my opinion, a leader needs to say what needs to be said and doesn't sugarcoat the truth. If you look at my Facebook page and scroll back to 2011, you can see that even when I had no money and no skills, I had heart. I was leading by example and building a following from day one in this business.

If they can't replace you, guess what? They will pay you and pay you well. This concept simply makes sense. And when things make sense, they make dollars. Find a need in the marketplace and fill it, gain the skills and master the basics in your field, and strive to be irreplaceable. You are cable of mastering the Law of Compensation by simply following the above guidelines, and, when you do, you will be greatly rewarded.

The idea of commitment is easy, but seeing it through is difficult. It's very easy for someone to be excited for a few weeks or even a few years. It takes a huge commitment and the heart of a champion to stay excited until you complete your goal. When I study top earners, it is absolutely astonishing to see how many of them lost focus, made up excuses, or were victims of being rich and lazy, or, in other words, becoming content.

One of my "You Tube mentors", Jim Rohn, says *"For things to change, you must change. Don't wish it was easier, wish you were better."*

My personal favorite from Rohn is *"Successful people do what unsuccessful people don't want to do."*

The idea of commitment is probably one of the easiest things to understand. You know exactly what it takes to accomplish your goal, right now, this very second—you just haven't made the decision yet to commit to this goal until the job gets done.

Abraham Lincoln once said, "Commitment is what transforms a promise into reality." Whether it's committing to eating an apple a day, running seven miles a week, or prospecting five new people every time you leave your home, you must understand that commitment is the only way to see results. *True commitment is doing what you said you were going to do, even when the emotion is gone.*

Every year most companies hold at minimum an annual convention. People from all over the world travel to these conventions to get trained, motivated, inspired, be around like-minded individuals, and, above all, make a commitment to building their businesses stronger than ever before. It's astonishing to me how many people make a commitment, set a goal, and, then, two weeks or two months later, they are back in their same routine, getting their same poor results, and making their same crappy excuses.

I challenge you to get committed and stay committed to your dreams and goals. Stop being affected by other people's actions and other people's opinions. Let them think and say what they want. It's funny, because all these critics who attempt to bring people down don't even have a plan—all they have is a critique. Stay focused, stay excited, and stay committed. I was told by a mentor that it takes 21 days for a habit to form. That's only three weeks. Can you eat healthy for 21 days straight? Can you commit to doing one presentation a day for 21 days or talking to one new person a day for 21? Let me be honest here: if you say that you can't, that's total and utter crap.

> *You CAN commit, you CAN decide to make it happen, and you CAN make it to your goals and dreams. Make the commitment today. It WILL be worth it.*

Bob Proctor has to be one of the most interesting men I've ever had the pleasure to know and work with. He cares about people. He could have comfortably retired decades ago, yet he still travels all over the world, helping people better their lives and getting people where they want to go. He's now over 80 years old, but he possesses the energy of an excited 18-year-old college kid hyped up on energy drinks. If you're not familiar with Bob, get familiar with him. If you haven't studied his information, study it, because his information changed my entire life.

Alex Morton Facebook post
December 13, 2013 • Chicago, IL •

There will be haters, there will be doubters, there will be non believers, & then there will be YOU, proving them wrong &.. more importantly proving yourself right. #ChaseYourDreams

Alex Morton Facebook post
December 8, 2014 • Toronto, Canada •

If someone isn't in sync, in alignment, on the same wavelength, frequency as you are with your goals, dreams, aspirations, & life's purpose then CUT THEM OUT OF YOUR LIFE immediately!!

There are billions of people on earth go out & surround yourself with people who are striving to do more, become more, & elevate their lives!! Drop the stagnant, time wasting, excuse making, cry babies, & lazy people who have settled for average & find WINNERS!!!!
#Immediately

CHAPTER 9

AMATEURS COMPETE, CHAMPIONS DOMINATE AND CONTINUALLY DEVELOP

You are either a winner or have not yet figured out how to win. I don't believe in losers, failures don't exist in my book, and I don't believe in giving too much time and energy to competition.

One of my best-kept secrets is that I do not pay attention to what the competition around me is doing, what they are thinking, how they are building their business, or how they are living their lives. It's an enormous distraction, and does not add value to your life.

Most people in the workplace, business world, and life in general are always comparing themselves to everybody else. I'll admit, I used to be one of those people. I would always observe how the competition is playing, what they were up to, how they were doing, until I drove myself crazy. Then, I realized that there is always someone dominating a given space. Whether it's sports, real estate, network marketing, or lawyers, there is usually always a dominating force running the industry or game.

It didn't take me long in my career to realize that in order to win big, I was going to have to hustle hard and go above and beyond with my energy and effort if I was going to dominate. When I joined my company, I was 21 years old, naive, and hungry as hell for success. There were two or three guys already in the company, and they were doing pretty well for themselves at a young age. Today, I am close friends with them; however, back then (being a 21-year-old dummy), I viewed them as competition, instead of colleagues. The day I stopped competing and made a firm decision to dominate was the day it all changed for me.

What I want to do now is explain the steps I took to launch my career and blast into momentum. As you read the next several paragraphs, I want you to think about the underlying principles I used. Once again, this isn't me speaking on theories or imagination, this is me telling you the exact things I did to explode my business and, in turn, earn over $1,000,000.

When I was new to the company, I became a sponge. I went to all the trainings I could, listened to all the audios I could get my hands on, and I studied video after video after video. I looked at the big money earners, and I observed exactly what they were doing, because I figured that if I could somehow duplicate their strategies, I could win big, just like them.

There were two individuals, in particular, who I really modeled myself after. In my business, we make a lot of presentations, whether it's a hotel event, private business reception, or a one-on-one at a local Starbucks. If you want to make a lot of money in this business, you've got to get really good at the presentation, and I mean really good.

I observed two primary components that went into creating and executing an effective presentation: the content and the delivery. Once I figured out that if I could master the art of telling the story, relaying all of the content on the company, the CEO, the products, the opportunity, and, most importantly, what it could do for them, I knew I could make it big. I sought out the best speaker in the company, hypothesizing that if I studied the best speaker, I could become halfway decent, myself. I found the best speaker in the company and the one with the best story, and I began to study them like it was my job, and, eventually, it paid off.

Nobody is a born a phenomenal speaker, presenter, or vision caster. It startles me that so many people think people are born naturals at certain crafts. It is true that people are born with God-given talent, but what you must learn to understand is that hard work beats talent any day of the week.

I learned early on in my career that you can either learn from mistakes or mentors. At 21, just getting starting in being an entrepreneur, thank God I had mentors who showed me what was possible and gave me the wisdom I needed to not only survive, but thrive. My advice for you is that you immediately go find someone who has exactly what you desire in life, listen to them, and take all-out, massive, immediate action.

Alex Morton
November 28, 2013 • Henderson, NV •

Thanksgiving is a time to reflect & give thanks to those who have made a positive impact on your life.

This past year has been crazy. I've had the privilege of traveling to dozens of cities, states, countries, meeting thousands of people, experience crazy stuff, & had the honor to impact other people's lives. I want to say I am THANKFUL to all my friends & family who have been there for me through thick & thin. Everyone who has supported me in this journey, in my business & watching on the sidelines, I appreciate you more than you'll ever know.

To everyone out there in the Universe who has connected with me, whether its been through phone, text, email, Facebook, twitter, Instagram.. I read all the messages & truly appreciate all the love & support & I am THANKFUL for each one of you. Means the world. To my team and crossline who follow our team's lead.. From the newest members to our ambassador leaders. I am honored, blessed, & THANKFUL to be able to serve you as your leader. You have my word I will never stop, never slow down, never be content, & never, ever stop working to help YOU get to where you all want to go, get some rest today because starting tomorrow 4th quarter push is on, & I'm talking ALL OUT massive action leading up to Vegas convention.

Love you guys, straight up die for y'all.
Life is short. Treat people right. Work hard. Go after your dreams. & above all, be humble, be hungry, & be THANKFUL.
Happy Thanksgiving 2013.
Love y'all.

CHAPTER 10

THE STRANGEST SECRET

I went from being broke-as-a-joke to speaking on stages all over the world, earning thousands per week, in a blink of an eye, and I wanted to know what the hell happened. Leading up to this point, I've told you stories about people close to me who defied the odds, went for it, and followed my success system. I have given you philosophies, what to focus on, how to set goals, how to develop that winning mindset, and how to go out there dominate your space.

In this chapter, I am going to dive deep into the exact things that literally changed my entire life. I want to warn you that some of this information may seem a little weird, crazy, and maybe even absurd. I felt the exact same way when I first discovered this material and began to realize that all successful people follow the same rules and play the same game.

My curiosity to find "the secret" eventually turned into a complete obsession. Every time I got in the car, I listened to personal development recordings. Every morning and every night, I began studying videos. Any time I got my hands on a book, I would demolish it.

All my life, I had been told that you had to be very smart to make a lot of money. I quickly found out that's just not true, because I know I am not that smart, and I am earning a lot of money. I was hungry to figure out what happened to me. I knew if I could figure out what happened to me, I could help a lot of other people stop struggling and start winning in their lives.

I was on YouTube one day, skimming through personal development videos, and I came across a specific one by Earl Nightingale, entitled "The Strangest Secret". The description of the video read:

This phenomenal message was first played for a group of salespeople at Earl Nightingale's insurance agency. They were extremely excited. Word of it spread like wildfire, and everyone who heard it was positively moved into action. Requests for the recording of the message came pouring in—thousands of requests per week. Within no time, more than 200,000 people had called, written, or just walked right into Earl's office to request a copy of their own. As years went by, that number soared above 1,000,000. By 1956, Earl Nightingale had already soared to successful heights as a Network radio announcer: the voice of Sky King; and host of his own daily radio and television show. Expanding his horizon, he bought a small Life Insurance company, insuring it's success by giving encouraging, inspiring, motivational talks to his sales staff. Then because he was going to be away, Earl wrote and recorded on a record, an essay which could be played during his absence. He called it THE STRANGEST SECRET. The response to the message had such an impact on the staff that requests for copies to share with friends and families grew. Columbia Records filled the requests and with in a short period of time sales soared to over a million copies, earning a Gold Record the first and only spoken word record to ever read Gold! Today, more than 40 years later, The Strangest Secret remains one of the most powerful and influential messages ever recorded. It continues to transform the lives of everyone who hears and heeds it. Prescription for success: listen or read twice a month for the next ten years, then once a month forever.

You can probably guess what happened next: I began to play it over and over and over again, on endless loop. I listened to this audio recording over 100 times in the year 2013, because it got me thinking differently, and it got me in tune with what caused my soar to success.

I am going to break this audio down into sections and explain Nightingale's ideas in my own words, because I believe I will help it make more sense to you. The first several times I listened to the damn thing, I had no idea what he was talking about.

Since I have listened to it countless times, I am able to give you an explanation that you will be able to immediately apply:

The beginning of the audio starts off with this insane statistic: out of 100 individuals who start working towards their goals and dreams at age 25, and every single one of them wholeheartedly believes in themselves, at the age of 65, only five of them have accomplished what they set out to do. Take a look around you. Look at your peers, your colleagues, your friends, your teammates, your family... have most of them really gotten the life they dreamt about growing up? Did they fall victim to dream-stealers or get swallowed up by the system?

Imagine yourself on your deathbed. Around you stands all of your goals, dreams, and aspirations. They are all looking at your with big, bold eyes, and they are saying, "We came to you, we came to you to become realities here on earth. You never went after it, you never pursued us, and now we will die with you forever!"

Nightingale said that so many people had and have such big and great intentions to do wonderful things and accomplish a great deal here, on Earth, but, when push comes to shove, most never amount to doing what they intended on doing.

You must understand at this very second that we live in the most blessed time in human existence! We live in an era that mankind has work towards, dreamed up, and sacrificed many things to reach. With today's unlimited reservoir of resources and unlimited rivers of knowledge, we are more than ever capable of accomplishing anything and everything we set our mind to.

Nightingale said that after 65 years of life, only 1 percent of people are wealthy, 54 percent are broke, 5 percent will still be working, 4 percent will be financially independent, and 36 percent will be dead. You're probably asking yourself the same thing I was asking myself a few years ago: How in the hell do I become that one percent? Throughout this book, I have offered you a guide to becoming that one percent, and, in the coming pages, you will learn even more to help ensure that you become that one percent.

Nightingale defines success as "the progressive realization of a worthy ideal". He goes on to say that success can come in many forms, not just financial. A lot of times we think of the word "success" and immediately think about money, cars, clothes, homes, and other materialistic possessions. Success is not the material, he urges, but the progressive realization of a worthy ideal. Success is the first-grade teacher who teaches children because that's what she wanted to do, the mother who raises her kids, the man who becomes an entrepreneur and starts his own company, and the college student who pursues her passion as a heart surgeon.

Next, he discusses goals. People who succeed, he says, do so because they know exactly where they are going. It truly is that simple. People who don't accomplish what they want and continue to fail believe that their lives are shaped by exterior forces and circumstances beyond their control, when, in fact, our lives are shaped by goals and knowing the laws of success.

Nightingale illustrates his point through a metaphor about two different ships. The first ship has a crew, a captain, and a mapped out plan to get to where it's going. It will reach its destination 99/100 times. The second ship has no crew, captain, or map, and it will, most likely, get nowhere.

This is what "beginning with the end in mind" is all about.

To get to a destination, you must first know where you are going. Nightingale goes on to say that it's the same thing with human beings, except here it's rigged not to prevent the strong from winning, but to prevent the weak from losing.

You see, the Universe actually wants us to live our dreams and accomplish our goals. I am about to tell you exactly what "The Strangest Secret" is. You may be surprised, startled, or even skeptical. I assure you that by the end of this section you will know exactly what it is, how to harness it, and how to use it to your advantage immediately.

WE BECOME WHAT WE THINK ABOUT (THAT'S IT)

Earl Nightingale says, "This is 'The Strangest Secret'! Now, why do I say it's strange, and why do I call it a secret? Actually, it isn't a secret at all." He relates that the "secret" was used by the earliest wise men, and it appears again and again throughout the Bible. Very few people, he says, have learned it or understand it, which is why it's strange and remains a secret.

The mind is a very powerful thing, and capable of just about anything. Have you ever heard, "If you can believe it, you can achieve it?" Well, that's exactly right. If you have negative thoughts, you will get negative results. If you have positive thoughts, you will get positive results. Think of your mind as an open field in which to plant crops that you water and grow. The mind works the same way. You can plant thoughts of positivity—helping people, great health, wealth, and prosperity, or you can plant thoughts of negativity—losing, bad health, and scarcity. The mind does not care what you plant. Whatever you plant, whatever you harvest, will eventually grow, whether it is good or bad.

Nightingale said, " We become what we think about." If you think about a goal, you will reach it; whereas, if you do not have a goal and do not know where you are going, you will, naturally, have thoughts of confusion, anxiety, fear, and worry, and you will create a life full of those things. If one thinks about nothing, he says, one will become nothing.

Nightingale said, "The moment you decide on a goal to work toward, you're immediately a successful person — you are then in that rare group of people who know where they're going." Once you are one of these people, you are in the top five percent of people. His powerful closing still sticks with me today, "You have nothing to lose — but you have your whole life to win."

ACTION PLAN

What I would like you to do now is figure out exactly what you want and burn it into your mind. It's probably the most important decision you'll ever make for the rest of your life. Half the battle is making a firm decision on what you want.

Make a goal card, write your goals on the card, and read it over and over again, every single day, until it is burned into your mind forever.

Alex Morton Facebook post
November 15, 2013 • Lubbock, TX •

"Dude I don't understand why you still are working, flying everywhere, sacrificing time away from family.. If I was 24 making $1,000,000 a year I'd be on a beach counting money."

My reply- "You don't understand what we are actually trying to accomplish here.. It's about shifting the mindset of an entire generation from employee to entrepreneur. We want to be remembered, leave a legacy, change 1000's of lives. & we haven't even started yet. When I'm doing $500K a month I'll still be flying all over the world helping people.. The money is just a result of how many people we've helped." #YPR

Alex Morton FB post
November 12, 2013 • Orlando, FL •

I refuse to read the paper, magazines, watch tv anymore all I see/hear are so many people bitching, moaning, complaining about Obama, the government, the job market, debt, the economy, peoples lives... DO SOMETHING ABOUT IT & freaking CHANGE YOUR SITUATION.

You are a human being, if you don't like something about your situation, change it. It's that simple. There's no secret to success..You don't have to be smart that's BS all it takes is a little blood, sweat, sacrifice, work ethic, & tears. PERIOD.

Make a bold decision & go out today & MAKE IT HAPPEN. #ALLIN

CHAPTER 11

MASTERING SOCIAL MEDIA

I can still hear the dial-up sound from our home computer when my family first had Internet in the house, more specifically AOL. I vividly remember writhing impatiently while it took up to 10 minutes to connect to the Internet, my wait punctuated by the sounds of crackling and other annoying noises.

Our generation, Gen Y, is the first generation to literally grow up online. From Netscape Navigator, to Internet Explorer, to MySpace, Facebook, Twitter, and Instagram, we've watched the Internet change a lot in our lives.

If you take a second and really think about all of this, it's freaking nuts! Can you remember selecting your "Top 8" friends list on Myspace and changing your profile pic on Facebook a hundred different times, because you only got one picture?

The more I have submerged myself into and learned about social media, the more that I am realizing how powerful this tool really is to our lives and our businesses. Social media allow sus to create custom profiles about ourselves. Social media allows us to tell the world our story, to share with people what we're excited about, what we do for work, and what is going on in our social lives. Ultimately, it allows us to brand ourselves in any shape or form that we desire.

Social Media is the quickest and most efficient way to network online. In my business—like so many others—it's all about connecting with people. People will rarely buy anything from you unless they like you. Social media allows you to build a brand, gain an audience, and, eventually, develop a list of customers who love you so much that they feel obligated to buy something from you. I will share with you the secrets that enabled me to build a total "list" of over 100,000 real people who all opt into my social networks, follow me, and look to me for guidance and leadership.

The principles and guidelines I am about to share with you are very basic. Social media is always changing, growing, and evolving, so, because of that, I wanted to keep it short, sweet, simple, and give you action steps to take your social media game to an entirely new level.

Principle #1- BECOME A BRAND

When I started my business four years ago, I immediately began to utilize social media to my advantage. As a business owner in the social network marketing space, I knew that if I could build a powerful brand online, I would attract like-minded individuals who would want to join my business.

It all began with me posting, real, honest statutes about my opinions on certain subjects like education, business, and social issues. I've always been an outspoken individual, but, once I got on social media, I went crazy with it, and, in turn, so did my business.

Your social media is a glimpse into who you are, both as a professional and a person, so it's important to be honest with the world, and show people what you stand for and who you really are. Your credibility is really all you have at the end of the day. When developing your brand, think about the message you want to put out into the Universe and how you want to be portrayed. When building your brand, you want to focus on building a community of people who will turn into followers who like, trust, and respect you.

You want to develop a community of people who are genuinely interested in the content you are providing. The bottom line is that when you're building your brand, it is of paramount importance to be as genuine as you possibly can and to go into it with the intention of creating something that you can be proud of that is going to positively impact other people.

I am in the network marketing industry. Most of the content I write and the videos I create are centered around direct sales, personal growth, and network marketing.

ACTION PLAN

Write the name of the industry you are in on a sheet of paper and circle it. From that point, think of adjectives that describe your industry, both positive and negative. Think about the stigmas or stereotypes surrounding your industry's image. Get creative here—really peel back the onion and get to the core of what your industry is all about.

Now, think about which concepts you are skilled at and which tactics you've mastered, and jot those down. Something as simple as a "Video of the Week" or a "Tip of the Day" can help people really see who you are and what you're about, and your brand will start to form.

I realized that I was very good at inspiring other people to really take action in their lives. I could turn on my iPhone camera and deliver a message so powerful that someone across the world, who doesn't even speak English, could feel what I was saying.

If I had to sum up the way that the Alex Morton brand was built in one word, I would choose the word "CONSISTENCY." Some people in my industry will post a few good posts a week or create a video every few weeks. On the other hand, I post everything I do. I create daily motivational videos, upload pictures of all my travels, and use my posts to create hype and show the world my work ethic.

Personally, I am attracted by individuals who have insane work ethics. A major part of my business is recruiting other like-minded people who want to change their financial situations, so, a few years ago, I realized that if I was consistent enough with my brand, pushed enough content out there, and really got strangers to feel like they've known me for years, I could attract of a lot of great business partners and really take my business to a next level.

As a result, I attracted some of my best partners via all the various social media vehicles: Youtube, SnapChat, Instagram, etc. Here's the coolest part: they contacted me, not the other way around.

> *Your brand is you, and you are your brand. Be creative, be selective, be consistent, and be relentless.*

Principle #2- PUSH VALUE

Now that you know you can build a brand on social media, it is now important for you to know exactly what kind of content you are presenting to your community. When it comes to pushing valuable content, you must truly commit to being consistent. You must view yourself as an enormous billboard stretching from all corners of the earth, because, in essence, you are doing just that.

Every single thing you post online announces to the world who you are and what you believe in as a person. It is also an opportunity to showcase your wisdom, knowledge, and expertise on certain topics or in a specific field or industry.

Understand that you can reach 60 different people, in 60 different countries, in 60 seconds, through your computer. When you tweet, post a status, or upload a YouTube video, you are immediately sharing that content with the world. That is powerful, and, when you can harness that power, you influence thousands of people, gain a massive following, directly and indirectly recruit people into your business, eventually turn your following into a stream of income, and, most importantly, have the power and privilege to impact people's lives for the better. Not only that, it's a crazy amount of fun.

When posting on social media, your ultimate goal is to add value to people's lives, to help them reach their desired goals and dreams, to teach them what you know, so they can implement your knowledge into their business. Before writing this chapter, I filmed a five-minute video on top of a rooftop on the beautiful island of Puerto Rico. The video was about my journey as an entrepreneur, the ups and down, and the trials and tribulations. I sent the user on an emotional roller coaster for five minutes and really spoke to their hearts. Keep in mind when "pushing value" to your followers and social media sites, it is important to connect with people on an emotional level, not just on their intellectual level. People like to be jolted, excited, woken up, stirred up, and enthusiastic. Your value-driven content needs to be powerful and give people a reason to always be coming back for more.

> *Post with a Purpose.*

Don't just upload pictures of the food you're eating and your outfit of the day. Before posting on any social media ask yourself, How is this going to be perceived by the user? What message am I trying to convey? What do I want the end result or major takeaway to be?

Every time I compose a post or shoot a video, I begin with the end in mind. I know exactly what my main points are going to be, I know the exact emotions I want to evoke in everyone watching, and I always end the post or video with a call to action.

Unlike many people who utilize social media to build their businesses, I don't plan my posts in advance. Instead, the ideas, concepts, messages come to me, and I feel inspired to share them with the world. I rarely rehearse, and the reason why my content is so compelling is that it is real. I don't sugarcoat anything.

I suggest you sit down today and start writing some posts. Write about what motivates you, what inspires you, talk about your journey as an entrepreneur, and focus on some simple steps that can help the user have a positive result / experience in their business. Adding value to others online comes very easy once you understand that people love to be educated and entertained, and realize that people want what you have. The online world is an amazing platform for you to help people get to where they want to go. Post with purpose, and post with the intent to change people's lives. If you're truly genuine, you will do great, and people will always be coming back for more.

Principle #3- RESPECT ALL

The online and social media world can most definitely seem like the Wild, Wild West at times. People have strong opinions on all sorts of topics, and, as a professional, we must respect everyone's viewpoints. If someone posts something that rubs you the wrong way it is important to not engage in trash-talking or starting online wars. Only amateurs engage in arguments and start fights in the cyber world. Professionals keep it classy. Constructive criticism and voicing your opinion is one thing, but being abrasive and vulgar is another.

When I say "respect all", I am talking about everyone's opinions on all subjects. We all come from different backgrounds, and we were all raised on a different set of morals and values, so it only makes sense that we would have different opinions on different subject matters.

The best way to win an argument is to not have one in the first place. Be respectful to anyone who comments on your material or voices their opinions on it. Answer people's questions politely and always have them leave your page in a good mood.

In my career, there have been so many situations in which I truly wanted to go off on an individual, prove them wrong, and start a ferocious argument. I chose to be the "bigger man" and just agree to disagree. You want to be known in the online world for voicing your thoughts and views, but you also want to be known for being respectful to everyone in the online community. If you can commit to this, it will help you build an even more powerful brand, and you will be respected throughout the online world.

The steps to mastering social media are just like the steps to success. They are easy to do and also easy not to do. It's up to you to make the correct decisions when building your brand, pushing value, and respecting all members of the online world. We live in such a connected world that social media has now turned into the largest playground mankind has ever seen.

We have the power to change people's lives through valuable content. In my career, I have touched hundreds of thousands of lives because of my pictures, posts, and videos. You have the exact same power, and also the exact same responsibility.

> *My wish for you is that you become a master of social media, build an enormous brand, create and push out extremely valuable content, that you genuinely want to help people change their lives, and that you absolutely crush it in your business in the online world!*

Alex Morton FB post
September 26, 2013 • Winchester, Nevada •

Back @ it baby!! 30 day tour, 2 countries, 8 states, 50 cities!! Time to change some lives & help my team all get to the next level!! I land at 5:30, & we have 3 home events lined up for tonight!! Me & big daddy Josh bringing the thunder & lightning!!!!!!
#AZBound #CanIGetaRACKKEMMMM

Alex Morton FB post
September 25, 2013 •

I hate the words (downline upline crossline).. refer to your team as your family. That's what they are.. & thats what they always will be.
#YPR

CHAPTER 12

IT'S YOUR TIME

You know that nervous feeling when your heart is racing, and you get goosebumps up and down your body and sweat dripping down your forehead? All of those are signs that you are most certainly on the verge of greatness. If you have it right now, you are ready to go out there and make your first million.

Throughout this book I have given you laws of success and ways to grow yourself into a champion. You have learned how to cultivate a bulletproof mindset and an unstoppable intensity. You are probably fired up, on an emotional high, and also wondering what to do next. You are now passionate about your future, hungrier than ever for massive success, and ready to do whatever it takes.

Now, I will give you a plan of action, to bring all of the pieces together. Your rocket ship to take your life to the next level is now on the launch pad, fueled up, and ready to go. Let's launch this thing right now!

THE ULTIMATE SUCCESS FORMULA

1. You Must Know Your Outcome.

You must know your desired outcome before you even start. Take a few minutes, get into a rhythm of deep breathing, and see yourself accomplishing everything you've ever wanted. What does that feel like?

Imagine that you are looking at yourself five years down the road in the mirror. Are you happy with that person staring back at you? Visualize your day-to-day life. What are you doing on a daily basis? Who are the people you surround yourself with? What does your bank account look like? Your home? Your car? Your clothing? What kind of lifestyle are you living?

Having been an entrepreneur for over five years now, I have realized that everyone has a life, but very few have a lifestyle. Take a moment to feel what your dream feels like—your fantasy world that you truly want to create into reality Taste it, touch it, smell it, be in it. It is very important that before you launch your new life and obtain amazing levels of success that you know your outcome.

2. Know Your Reasons Why.

Why do you do what you do? What is your driving force? Why is your success an absolute must that you will achieve, no matter what obstacle, challenge, setback, or detour stands in your way? What will keep you fighting, crawling, and running your way through any setback? Why must you be an unstoppable force? Regardless of how big your new goals are, willpower will only take you so far. You need "WHY" power.

3. Take Massive Action.

You must immediately set C-type goals, develop a strategy, and go to work. How long will you need to go to work, sacrifice many things in your life, give up sleep, and work to exhaustion? You will need to take massive action until. Until what, you ask? UNTIL. Until the job gets done and you smash all the goals you set.

It is critical that you understand that nothing of great consequence has ever been achieved without massive, continuous action. If you take a look at many successful movie stars, musicians, and athletes, they almost all attribute 90 percent of their successes to all-out, massive, immediate action.

What I have figured out through the intense study and observations of highest achievers in the world and also becoming a millionaire by 25 is that anything and everything that is outstanding has come from brutally hard work and massive action. Plan your work, and, then, go work your plan. Do whatever it takes UNTIL the job gets done.

4. Know What You Are Getting.

You know your desired outcome, you know why you're about to go all in, and you now have an understanding that your goals and dreams are going to require massive action. It's now time to know what you're getting.

I am not telling you to be greedy; I am telling you that it's imperative to be working towards something. That "something" might be a fancy car, a big home, a dream vacation, retiring your mom, or walking away from your job. You must know what you are getting.

I suggest making a dream board. Get on the Internet and design your future with vivid pictures. Take those pictures, make a collage, and put it somewhere that you see it constantly and frequently. You're about to embark on an amazing, difficult, and grueling journey. You need to know what awaits you at the finish line, what you are receiving for all your hard work, and how your life is going to be like when you make it. Know what you are getting, and work your butt off to make it happen.

5. Accept The Fact That You Deserve Success.

This last and final step may seem a bit odd, but what I have found with many people is that they have limiting beliefs—for some reason, they don't believe that they even deserve success. Some people grew up in households in which they were taught to play it safe and stay in line—a household that believed that being successful was for other people. Some people were told all of their lives that they aren't good enough, smart enough, attractive enough, or skilled enough to achieve success.

Because of this they never take action. which results in an unfulfilled and unhappy life. I do not care where you come from, what color your skin is, what kind of financial upbringing you had—it doesn't matter! You are God's highest form of creation, capable and able to accomplish anything you want. Your past does not determine your future. YOU DESERVE SUCCESS!

TIME TO MAKE IT HAPPEN

It is now time to go for it. It is time to go make it happen. It is time to get excited about your life and get ready to rock and roll. It is time to charge in the direction of your wildest dreams and goals and pursue them with relentless ambition.

I have poured my heart, soul, secrets, principles, and mindset for success into you. Regardless of what industry you're in, job you have, or your current situation, you can immediately apply all of the things in this book and start to see and experience a massive change in your life and in your results. If you think big, you will get big. THINK BIG, DREAM BIG, BELIEVE BIG, AND ACHIEVE BIG. Do it now! RIGHT NOW!

Read the words below with intensity, tenacity, ferociousness, and conviction. Read it a minimum of three times, and, on each successive read, get more emotionally involved and intense:

I AM A CHAMPION.
I WILL LEAD, NOT FOLLOW.
I WILL BELIEVE, NOT DOUBT.
I WILL CREATE, NOT DESTROY.
I AM A FORCE DEMANDING SUCCESS.
I AM A CHAMPION.
I WILL DEFY THE ODDS.
I WILL WORK UNTIL I WILL ACHIEVE MY DREAM.
I AM A CHAMPION.

You are God's highest form of creation. You are destined for and deserve greatness, success, and abundance. Believe in yourself, and make it happen. I BELIEVE IN YOU! NOW, GO ATTACK THE WORLD, CHANGE PEOPLE'S LIVES, AND TURN YOUR DREAMS INTO A REALITY.

EPILOGUE

SUCCESS LEAVES CLUES- POSTS (REAL TIME) FROM THE JOURNEY THUS FAR

Alex Morton FB Post
December 9, 2012 • Tempe, AZ •

Show me any great victory, show me anyone who ever achieved greatness, & I will show you someone who became fully obsessed, turned into a fanatic in order to achieve what was desired. Most people give up, most people are too scared to step out of line, to go against the grain, to be different. That's why most people never achieve what they want. That's why most people are forced to live on the leftovers of highly successful people.

Be unreasonable, be dangerous, take calculated risks. If a group of people didn't become obsessed do you really think we'd have air travel, exploring space, have become such a powerful nation? Do you think championship teams are just "half in" or "just trying to win" MOST people just keep testing the waters temperatures, how about just jump the hell in.

Successful people see past the problem, the small setbacks, the adversity.

GO ALL THE WAY. Lets be honest, life is all about results. Don't accept excuses, no settling is allowed when you're GOING ALL THE WAY. Live & be in the NOW. Forget the past & don't focus on the future. Take actions immediately right now to design the life you want to live. Create your own reality. You want a private plane, a beach front condo, to retire your parents? You have to do what it takes to get there. STOP planning & START doing. Stop thinking, organizing, planning, developing.. & start doing! COMMIT FIRST & figure everything else out later.

See in school, most of your parents & family, media, & society look down on being different. Everyone must get an A, everyone must make a resume, everyone must get an internship, get a job. I remember growing up and hearing friends parents saying, "Well you guys just need to keep your head down ,chin up, save money, live under the radar, work hard & do what your told, every now & then your boss will throw you a bone or give you a raise." Not in my freaking house. You've got to be kidding me. Teachers telling me, well Alex people who are millionaires are "geniuses" ordinary people like all of us can't do the things they do. We need you to fill out this test, go see the guidance counselor so we can see what career you can go into & work for someone else. That's just NOT true. YOU are a human being & can do, achieve, become ANYTHING you want. The most successful look for ways to break traditions & design the future with forward thinking. Highly successful people don't give a damn about "how everyone operates & lives life & the middle class & people who gave up on want they truly wanted out of life.. They focus on how to improve the current situation & how to make their dreams come true. Heck, if you don't go after want you want.. You'll spend the rest of your life working for someone who did.

This is about life & forgetting all the low energy, small thinking, no dreaming, being average, getting a job, & FOCUSING on your mission, developing a high level of motivation, getting literally obsessed with what you want, becoming a goal focused individual & making everyone that comes into contact with you better. Make others better & help others achieve high levels of success. Nothing feels better than helping others.

Anyways.. You can't take the money with you. Success isn't what's in your bank account it's how many lives you can positively change, how many kids can you motivate to become their best, how many families can you help.. & how many people will truly show up at your funeral. Everyone deserves to live the life they want. Go out there & make it happen & literally mute, vaporize, forget the existence of small thinking, safe playing, negative, ignorant, dream stealing individuals.

Become so successful, become so great that they have no choice..
but to support you.

Happy Sunday. #YPR

Alex Morton FB post
November 21, 2013 at 8:23am • Columbus, OH •

Growing up you're taught to color in between the lines, follow the system, write your papers according to a rubric, teachers & parents measure ones intelligence by an exam score, a standardized test, letter grades on a paper.

At 17 I sat in a guidance counselors office where I was asked to "pick a career," I was told if I didn't improve my SAT score of 1490/2400 I wouldn't get into a good school, & that meant never find a good job, which meant make no money, which equaled a not so good life... So I was told.

Growing up thinking differently was actually wrong. We lose points for creativity, for deviating from the guidelines. I remember asking my chemistry teacher "how in the world is the periodic table of elements going to help me provide for my family one day?" I remember asking the point of pre calculus & the reasoning behind the professor making us memorize ancient art history. I was told "it teaches you how to think," "Alex just follow the damn rules & finish your homework on time.. IT'S JUST THE WAY IT IS.... So I was told.

Then you grow up & realize 90 percent of everything you were taught, most of the ideas & systems & methods were BS, & you realize the world truly is what you make it. & you realize anyone who have ever accomplished anything, did something amazing, broke the rules, fought the system, was unrealistic, advocated a change, & thought & acted different, acted with passion & excitement.

This isn't about an energy drink, or vitamin supplement, or BMW's, diamond watches, money.... THIS is about waking up & explaining to OUR generation, the millennials, that our parents & grandparents had it all wrong, they actually completely screwed up, their plan didn't work, I mean, turn on the news, ask mom & dad when they're retiring. Most people are in a prison except you can't see the bars. Slavery might have been abolished back in the day but its back in full force right in front of your face... OPEN YOUR EYES.

Wake up. I mean seriously wake your ass up & realize you can do whatever you want. You control your destiny. Not some test score, not the opinion of your college guidance counselor. YOU control YOU. & ill tell you what.. WE have the vehicle. We have the vehicle right now in the palm of our hands to change everything, to spark change, to lead a revolution, to help people see the light. One day when we're on our death bed we won't regret what we did, we'll regret what we didn't do. The chances we didn't take, the shot we didn't even shoot... Let's freaking make it happen & go down in history. Leave a LEGACY of helping people & achieving GREATNESS.

(This is what happens when I'm alone in a airport terminal for 30 minutes lol)
#YPR #Cannnnaaaaaddaaaa

Alex Morton FB post
December 25, 2013 • Henderson, NV •

I want to say a THANK YOU to everyone who has been apart of my life this past year. It's definitely been one crazy ride. Thanks for all the support, encouragement, & love!!

To my team, who is now my FAMILY, Words can't describe what you all mean to me. I am honored & blessed to be able to help lead you all through this journey. I promise to NEVER stop working until everyone is where they want to be. 2014 I will work harder than I did in 2013. More flights, More drives, More calls, More leading by example, less breaks, & no sleep! Love you guys so much & cannot wait to get back to work. Swear on everything I know 2014 is YOUR year!!

To my business family, corporate staff, & all my crossline family!! I love you guys thanks for all that you do. All my meetings will continue to be open for everyone, calls, trainings, travel schedules.. As the water rises so do ALL the boats! Thanks for all the twitter, facebook, instagram messages, those heart felt messages mean more than any pay check. WE are in this together, as one company. Family.

Looking to go to Australia, Mexico, Canada, Europe, South America, Africa, Asia & help the #YPR teams grow in 2014.. Get ready!! I'm only 24, I know I don't always make the best decisions, I know sometimes I don't think before I act, sometimes I get out of control, definitely not perfect. I'm working on it.. For a 24 year old kid, I think I'm doing pretty good..

Happy Holidays & Happy New Year. Enjoy the time with your family!
2014 will be EPIC!!!
#HolidayMessage2013

Alex Morton FB post
December 15, 2013 • Mifflin, OH •

Just got finished with Columbus, Cleveland, & Youngstown events!! Sitting here on the 4 hour drive back to Columbus to catch the 9am flight to Denver... Wanted to share some thoughts, it's Sunday night..

Time to think & reflect a little & get prepared for a huge week: There are ALOT of people struggling. There are ALOT of families struggling to put food on the table, keep the lights on, keep the family under one roof. Got the opportunity to personally talk to some Cleveland kids/ parents & some people in Youngstown.. Hearing things like "Man if you grow up in this city or these streets you don't have many options.. Most sell dope to pay bills, work fast food, & then get into a steel mill or work for G.E. I spoke to a kids father.. Worked 7am-7pm for the last 26 years & NOW is earning $66,000/year. Another kids dad working corporate for 25+ years & now is being told he can't afford to retire, 16 year old girl raising a child on her own.. & using our company as her vehicle. Some scary stuff out there!!!! YOU can make a difference!!!!!

Don't take this opportunity for granted.. This isn't a game, this isn't a side thing, this isn't a hobby.. This is an opportunity to make an impact on humanity.. To literally change families lives.. To better people's situations.
You should see the faces I see of gratitude & feel the hugs from kids moms who are thankful someone actually cares about the well being of their kid...

Money comes & goes, material items are cool.. But at the end of the day what LEGACY are you leaving? How many people are going to show up to your funeral??? How many people behind closed doors talk highly of you because what you've done for them?

If you are apart of this phenomenal company than I highly suggest you splash some cold water on your face & realize you should feel obligated to work hard.. $100/ month $2000/month $6000/month or $1,000,000 a year... Doesn't matter. Go out into the world with the intention of helping others, that's all, the $$$ will follow. FOCUS ON THE VISION & THE MISSION & not on the commission.

The good $$$ will follow the good heart with the right intentions. Sorry for the novel I just know ALOT of people (including me) get so caught up in $$$, cycles, ranks, we lose sight of what we ACTUALLY are accomplishing. If you think this is about "health & wellness" you've lost your mind. This is 100%, no questions asked, no arguing.. A REVOLUTION.
DENVER!! See ya soon!!!!
#LegacyOverCurrency

Alex Morton
December 10, 2014 •

Heard tonight through the grapevine someone say, "ALEX ONLY CARES ABOUT THE PEOPLE WHO ARE MAKING HIM MONEY."

Very interesting statement. Lets take a deeper look....
MYSELF, along with ANY & EVERY leader in our profession worth a damn, any type of value, anyone who understands leadership,

CARES ABOUT EVERYONE AT ALL TIMES and displays that when appropriate. However, I have been trained by a man who has earned $36,000,000 in his career & another man who has been studying the laws of achievement and the laws of success for over 50 years who is probably earning $250,000 a week currently at 80 years old.
This is what they said regarding this subject.

"Alex, you must care about everyone on your team regardless of what effort he/she is displaying or the results they are getting. HOWEVER, you MUST work with, spend time with, build relationships with, coach, train, mentor, those individuals who are going ABOVE & BEYOND, the ones STRIVING FOR MORE, the guy who is doing WHAT IT TAKES to make it. You only can spend so much time with so many people, choose wisely. It's not your business it's their business. If they want to make excuses and bitch let them go make a resume & obtain financial freedom that way. You're at the point now where even if you donated $100,000 to charity A, there will be a group of people scorning you for not giving the money to charity

B. The second you try to get everyone to like you, get everyone to accept you, is the second you will lose control and begin a downward spiral. Give your time and devotion to the people you believe can do what you're doing and hopefully one day do it even better than you. Make people earn your damn time just how you had to prove yourself and earn your mentors time."

YOU, I, US cannot feel guilty about someone on our team not getting their desired results. Today in the seminar learning from the brightest man I've ever met he told the class (KEEP IN MIND THIS SEMINAR IS $15,000 A PERSON, THATS NOT A TYPO, $15,000 A PERSON) he said, "Whether you leave here and apply this knowledge or not, whether you get the results your looking for or not, I refuse to feel guilty about it. I am teaching you everything you need to know in order to accomplish anything you want, what you do with it is up to you."
IF IT'S TO BE IT'S UP TO ME.!!!!!!

Alex Morton FB post
December 29, 2014 • Spring Valley, NV • Edited •

As we approach the end of 2014 I would like to say THANK YOU to all the amazing people that have motivated, coached, mentored, & helped me become a better person this year. Although most definitely not perfect, I feel I grew this year.

I traveled to over 25 states, 12+ countries, & flew roughly 267,000 miles. To everyone who greeted me with open arms, invited me into your homes, & all the moms who made me home cooked meals, I appreciate you all. Being on the road for 2-4 weeks at a time was tough, but well worth it to see our team flourish.

To our amazing DREAM TEAM INTERNATIONAL, now having active affiliates & customers in all 50 states, over 30 countries, all I can say is thank you for your hard work, commitment to growth, tenacity to succeed & reaching your full potential, your priceless friendships, & most importantly the opportunity & blessing to be considered your leader. I will never stop working, growing, becoming better, developing new content, & in 2015 we will have our best year yet. To our present 19 six figure+ earners & leaders, I pray you go into the new year with the right attitude, positive mindset, leaving all bullshit excuses at the door, & a will to win. There's no room for blame & excuses with winners. There are no issues or problems except in your own minds. It begins with you & ends with you. Your thoughts control your feelings your feelings control your actions & your actions control your results.

We have hungry & driven leaders looking to fill spots on the leadership totem pole & they are damn good & damn motivated. To the up & coming leaders (GOLD-EXECUTIVE) it's your time now, the throne is open for the taking, the torch is waiting to be passed, make 2015 your teams breakout year & pursue your goals with relentless action & keep leading from the heart. You know exactly who you all are & I am SO proud of each and every one of you.

To my mentors (although some of you will not see this) Tony Robbins, Les Brown, Jim Rohn, John C Maxwell, Bob Proctor, Darren Hardy, Eric Thomas, my Parents, Eric Worre, Nick Sarnicola, Holton Buggs, Tim Herr, Grant Cardone & many more... THANK YOU for paving the way, educating me & showing the world what is possible once all doubt is eliminated & unwavering belief takes over. Because of all of you I know I can achieve whatever the hell I desire in life & help others do the same.

To every member of our profession, people that choose to follow me, hungry entrepreneurs around the world: In 2015 I will do everything in my power to provide more content, more value, some new recently learned trainings on the mind, & more hype motivation to help you get closer to your goals & dreams.

My wish is that 2015 is everyone's best year yet. Spend time with those you love, cherish the moments, pursue your goals & dreams with relentless action, don't listen to the small minds & cowards, & never, ever, give up.
HAPPY NEW YEAR.
#Alex Morton

Alex Morton Facebook Post September 17, 2014 at 9:40am • Holesovice, Czech Republic •

Network Marketers-
People do NOT buy your product or service.
They do NOT buy your magical lotion, potion, juice, dried fruit, shakes, candles, soaps, $99 or $499 boxes of air, or body wraps...

What they do buy is YOU.

There is no physical way in a 30 minute presentation they honestly fully grasp your compensation plan or all the benefits of your product/service or lack there of.

They FEEL GOOD about YOU, they TRUST YOU, they LIKE YOU, & they think that YOU can HELP them. YOU are your best asset & worst detriment. The question here is would YOU follow YOU? Would YOU trust YOU? Are you worth following?

YOU must work on yourself. Become sharp, crisp, clean, well spoken, attractive, friendly, confident, nice. YOU must develop what I like to call MAGIC. The best leaders in our profession have MAGIC. When they walk into a room no words need to be said everyone is attracted to them like magnets, they can make strangers feel like best friends, & they give off an Aura so powerful that people just want to be in their presence.

Your company, brand, product, service, it's YOU.
The biggest question here is would YOU buy YOU?
#AlexMortonMindset.com

June 25, 2013 at 10:12am • Henderson, NV •

You go to school for 12 years from k-12, then another 4 years in college. & not one damn teacher tells you how to make money. But they'll shove science, math, literature down your throat. & if you ask (which I did everyday) "how's this going to help me make $$$?" they respond "alex that's not the point, we're teaching you how to think critically, pay attention." Yeah that makes all of 0 sense to me when kids have $50,000 of loans or moms working 2 jobs to pay for school. Then kids graduate (10/12 of my best friends) doing exactly what mom & dad & teachers told em to do... & can't get a job.. Or they're trading time for money making $50K a year after taxes you're screwed. Yet 3% of this nation owns 97% of the wealth & 99.8% of OUR parents can barely afford to put food on the table, most families are taking 1 vacation a year, crappy home, crappy health, crappy car, average lifestyle, #1 reason for divorce in America is financial issues.

Then we get older.. We just learn to accept being average & never accomplishing our big goals and dreams.

I remember in HS my counselor stressing how important a SAT & GPA is.. telling me if i didn't go to a good school it'd be tougher to get a good job. Then in college my counselor tells me "that's just the way it is, you go to school to get a job to work for someone else to retire & enjoy a few years Alex."

Yeah that's what YOU do. That's what the 99% do. That's why their bitching moaning complaining about their BS lives & never accomplish a damn thing. Forget being average & living "a nice good life below your means."

Do something great, live a crazy ass life, make money, give back, help people, travel, do what you want, have no regrets, & don't look back.
#YoungPeopleRevolution

Alex Morton
June 30, 2015 • Phoenix, AZ, United States •

I recently had a top leader/friend in another company tell me:

"Alex I am definitely a fan of your work but sometimes you come off a bit cocky with a little ego sometimes."

I replied, "I think you're getting confused with my unwavering belief in myself & my mindset that I will do whatever it takes to help my team win. All the great leaders whom I have studied (Alexander The Great, MLK, Lombardi, Lebron, MJ, Kobe,etc) have all had an edgy side. A side that showed the world that they aren't scared one bit & regardless of the obstacle in front of them they were going to find a way to win."

I teach my people (who show the immense desire) to be confident, have conviction, & develop an unwavering belief that you're going to the top of the mountain or they'll find you dead on the side. People follow people who are determined, sold out, & on a mission.

There's a distinct difference between being confident & cocky/ego. Confidence is knowing you're capable of being the best & getting the job done, respecting all & fearing none, & working on your craft.

Ego/cocky is walking in a room & giving off a vibe that you're better than everyone, not giving people the time of day, & acting like a compete tool / D Bag.
That's my 2 cents.
#LetsGoooooBabyyyyyyy
#BeConfident

Alex Morton
July 1, 2015 •

You should be pondering the question...
"How can I turn my annual income into my monthly income?"
Not...
"Where I am partying this weekend?"
#THINK

Alex Morton added a new video.
July 13, 2015 •

Been going hard today since 5am. Shot over 1000 photos, 19 videos, & banged out 5 closing calls for my Network Marketing business.

Just shot this video for all of you because I want you to know that the journey to success is a wild ride. Be prepared to give up sleep, sacrifice some 'fun', lose some friends, gain some friends, have strangers hate you, even more adore you, get angry, get pissed, get happy, cry yourself to sleep, & eventaully live your dreams.
#DormRoom2Millionaire
I Believe In YOU!!!!

ALEX MORTON
July 19, 2015 • Schaumburg, IL, United States •

Very powerful image here of the worldwide known artist Eminem reading "How to Win Friends & Influence People." It's mind boggling how the industry of "personal growth" is almost kept secret from the masses. Now I could go on a rant & share my opinion on why that is but I won't. Mostly everyone you know who has obtained a massive amount of success has & continues to personally develop. I have seen videos of JayZ & Kanye discussing "Think & Grow Rich," Serena Williams has had Tony Robbins personally coach her for years, Big Sean, Jim Carrey, Diddy, 50 Cent, etc have talked about the power of visualization & personally developing.

The foundations of this industry (Vision, Driving Force, Purpose, Goal Setting, Work Ethic, Influence, Persuasion, Public Speaking) should be STAPLES in our educational system. Where in the hell is a kid going to use calculus, the memorization of random facts, & the periodic table of elements, at least the masses. They can Youtube everything.

The world has changed. You can find the answer to any question within 5 seconds on Google, get picked up within 5 minutes by an Uber, & go anywhere in the world & stay in a home powered by Air Bnb. Times have changed, the way we earn money has changed, and there will be a massive change of wealth in this world the next 10 years. Adapt, Evolve, Advance, Get Better, or just lay down & die.. That's life in 2015. You're no longer competing with Mr 2300 SAT score & Mr Warton School of Business graduate even though I'm a firm believer you can't TEACH entrepreneurship. You're competing with kids in Bangladesh, smart Asians who will work 18 hours a day to beat your ass in business, & kids in India who can speak 4 languages by 15 years old.

Keep partying, keep smoking, keep being a dumb dumb & you'll get slaughtered in the business world by people not necessarily more intelligent than you but people who will sacrifice it all to beat you. They aren't focused on reality TV or poppin bottles. They're focused on figuring out how to win.

I suggest getting your head in some books, flooding your mind with powerful audios, watch captivating videos, spend some money on transforming seminars. Or you can keep getting punished & slaughtered by people out working & out growing you. Feel like a worthless human & spend your (husbands boyfriends girlfriends wife's) hard earned money while you sit on your ass or go shopping all day while you probably have a nanny to raise your own darn children. OR take over your daddy's business which 7/10 times will be replaced by robots in the near future anyways. C'mon People.

Not a rant, just my personal thoughts. Agree to disagree if you choose. Bottom line is that I have been able to be around, learn from, & study people the top 3% & even the 1% and how they think, eat, breathe, act, operate differently than the 97% masses of sheep controlled by the media & the negativity all around us. "THEY" win because they learned, unlearned, & re learned how to WIN. Not just financially. But in significance, growth, contribution, love, & happiness. You can be filthy rich & be miserable. Study the 3% & do what they do. Stop listening to failures and get around some winners.

Register at AlexMortonMindset.com for the real information on how to change your freaking life. Not the fluffed up noisy garbage pouring into your minds 24/7. #GROW

Alex Morton
August 12, 2015 •

I want everyone to understand that this business takes time, energy, & effort. The road to success & greatness is a long winding road filled with potholes, broken bridges, bad weather, & many obstacles that you must overcome. I started my career in the Network Marketing profession in early 2011. I knew absolutely nothing about this industry, I never really accomplished anything of much consequence prior to this business, & to be honest I did not have a high level of skills. I was a 21 year old punk college kid only interested in when the next party was. If you're reading this message & you're 4,14,44,or 104 you must understand that regardless of which career or industry you enter into, the majority of the income earned is by the top 3%-5%.

So one must ask themselves, "how can I get into the top 5% of my company or profession?" The way to get there is by working harder & smarter than everybody else. I once heard you don't have to work hard to earn a lot of money, I don't buy that. The vast majority of ultra successful people that I have come across work hard, like really hard. But they also work smart.

Inside the Network Marketing profession it is most definitely a journey to the top. & the tricky part here is that you're never at THE TOP. I've observed that the best of the best in our profession work harder once they're making 7/8 figures than they did when they were broke. One of my mentors told me that anyone can get to the top but only a few can stay there. The main message here is that anyone can make it, anyone can be successful here, but what we do is easy TO DO, & also easy NOT TO DO. Anyone can make a list, learn an invitation, learn a script, host an event, sign up their dang cousins on some products, enroll some leaders. The secret is being CONSISTENT. The secret is doing something every single day to build your business and help your people. SO many networkers take days off when they shouldn't, make excuses when they shouldn't, & create made up beliefs & limitations inside of their heads to why they feel they cannot accomplish greatness. I've learned 95% of this business is between the ears, aka MENTAL.

The 2 major cornerstones of success are WORK ETHIC & ENTHUSIASM. Without these two things working in your favor you WILL NOT get to where you want to go in life. I don't care how "intellectually" smart you are, your degree, your upbringing, none of that matters. You must master EMOTIONAL INTELLIGENCE. You must be able to connect with people, relate to people, and have a heart to genuinely help people. The top earners in this profession all actually gain happiness in helping people. The ones running around concerned about their pay check, & their income, their rank, will NOT last long in this business OR their team will stop following them.

My first year in network marketing I earned an incredible $13,000. I got told no, I got made fun of, I got laughed at, I was called every name you could imagine, & I NEVER GAVE UP. I remember staring at the rank advancement chart (ask my college roommates) & just visualizing myself making it, on stage. I became obsessed with figuring it out & making it happen. You can look at my LinkedIN profile that I created in 2011 & I wrote "I will make $1,000,000 by 25." & I did it. Not because I'm special, because I refused to settle.

Do not give up on your dreams. Do not let people steer you

off course. Do not let your friends belittle you for trying something different, stepping out of your comfort zone, & going after your dreams & goals. Become a student of success. Become a sponge to information that can help you get better & in turn cause you to experience success. Seek out mentors, seek out people who know what they are talking about. Study them, copy them, obsess over what they do & then go do it.

You have greatness within you, GOD put you on earth for a purpose. If there is air in your lungs then you are not finished yet. Decide, commit, work hard, study, believe, & you will achieve anything you want.
#Focused

Alex Morton
August 28, 2015 •
The main principle that I've always preached is
WORK ETHIC.
6 planes in under 72 hours.
It's 4:16am
Don't tell your team what to do..
SHOW THEM.
#ServantDrivenLeadership

Alex Morton
September 4, 2015 •

Lesson from the journey: See & respect other people's perspectives.

Earlier in my career I used to only see things through my perspective, my goals, what I wanted, what I thought was the best way. This helped & hindered my leadership lid at the same time. If a young person didn't see the vision of becoming a millionaire I thought something was wrong with them. Sometimes I could cast a big enough vision for them to change their minds however I couldn't of been more wrong to only see it through "my lens."

It's important as a leader to see things through everyone's perspective. Sometimes it's tough to hear someone only wants an extra $500-$1000 a month, however your goals aren't their goals. Everyone has a different definition of success. We must all learn to respect it & encourage it. About 2 years or so ago I started looking at other people's choices, perspectives, & decisions through their eyes. It has changed everything for my business as well as life.

Also, it's very important to build a strong customer base. Often times in this business people tend to spend the majority of their time recruiting other distributors. I am a firm believer that a 10:1 customer to distributor ratio is wildly important. In our last 5 weeks in business the main focus has been customer acquisition & learning the ins and outs of retail sales. Build a strong customer base for real long term residual income!
#Leadership

Alex Morton
September 5, 2015 •

"Work harder on yourself than you do on your job; your income is directly related to your philosophy, not the economy; and for things to change, you must change."
-Jim Rohn

Network Marketing is one of the simplest ways to create wealth however it's very difficult to stick it out long term. SO many people are flash in the pan success stories. Getting "lucky or blessed" once upon a time & making some serious income short term. It's important to remember your "financial thermostat" is always working. If you're only worth $45,000 a year & all of a sudden you acquire $300,000. It's best you become worth $300,000 to the marketplace quick, or you'll soon be back to $45,000. You see, we always earn what we are. Our income is directly associated with the value we provide to the marketplace & the difficulty of replacing us.

So I must ask, how hard would it be to replace you? What do you bring to the table that's different than others? What's your specialized skill(s)?

One of the biggest things I've realized that had such a tremendous effect on my influence & leadership lid was continuously growing myself. Early on I thought personal development was a bunch of nonsense. But quickly I realized it was everything. We're in the business of growing people. How are we going to grow people if we're not growing ourselves? I have an intense personal development regiment. Do you? You should? If you see yourself as a 6 or 7 figure earner than you better acquire the skills & mindset of one.

"We are in the business of growing people. When you build the people, the people will build the business." #Focused

Alex Morton with Esther Morton and Len Morton.
September 13, 2015 •

Woke up this morning and decided to surprise my Grandparents and mom/dad/uncle by flying into Tulsa for a day & a half. I used to think getting super rich automatically made people happy. That's simply not the case.

Money is ONE of the keys to the kingdom, not THE key. Happiness to me is about creating memories with the people you love and care about.

Life is about GROWTH & figuring out a way to make this world a better place. I'm grateful to have found the vehicle and THE BEST way to make that happen.

A $100K car is only a $100K for 6 months and then it's just "a car." A $60K watch is only a $60K watch for 6 months and then it's just "a watch." Long lasting, strong, incredible relationships will always remain and last a lifetime.

"He was the poorest man in the world, all he had was money."
#ChaseThePurposeNotThePaycheck

Alex Morton
September 18, 2015 •

We don't believe in a 9 to 5.
We believe in from when our eyes open to when our eyes close.
#Focused
#4amHelllllllooooooooo

Alex Morton
September 16, 2015 •

Adversity either breaks you or makes you a RECORD BREAKER!!!!
#FIIIIIIIIIIRRRRRREEEDDDUUUPPP

Alex Morton at Detroit Metro Airport (DTW).
October 9, 2015 • Detroit, MI, United States •

Most people I come across want financial success, the nice big home, luxury cars, would love to travel the world and take care of their parents & loved ones. For the most part, the majority of the industry in my opinion truly does want to help people and change people's lives. The problem I constantly see is their commitment level doesn't correlate with their dreams. My advice to you is that you must either INCREASE YOUR COMMITMENT or DECREASE YOUR DREAMS. It's ok to dream big, it's ok to be confident about where you're headed. However, don't be a hypocrite. Don't tell yourself and the world you want to make 6 figures or be a millionaire and then get distracted by TV, instagram, sporting events, and not taking the simple, necessary steps to become a success story & "make it."

Moving forward, if you're asking yourself how to raise your commitment level.. Here's one simple concept I have committed to following to make sure my commitment is parallel to my dreams. MAKE, BUILD, CREATE, FOSTER, 5 NEW RELATIONSHIPS A DAY. Every single freaking day. If all you did was talk to 5 new people a day, that's

35/week, 140/month, 1680/year. Now if you eventually got all of these new people to view a tool, get to an event, participate in a 1on1 or 2on1, or hop on a 3way call with your upline, you'd be doing more than 98% of distributors in this industry. Let's say you close 1/3 of them as customers, preferred customers, or distributors, that's 560 NEW people in your business a year. Good Gosh Ole Mighty would you be seeing some success!

Continuing, you might be asking yourself how do you create those new relationships? Do you ever go out to eat? Go to the grocery store? Gym? Bar? Club? Play Sports? Go to the mall? On a bus? On a train? On a plane? Are you a human being with a mouth and a pair of ears? Ladies and Gentlemen go out into the marketplace and meet people. Be friendly, ask questions, get to know people, & my biggest secret is to always have a BIG FAT SMILE on my face. When you smile at someone they simply light up. Give people compliments, make others feel real good. If you have a 5 minute conversation with me, male or female, regardless of age, I guarantee you're smiling and filled up with positivity by the end of it.

GET COMMITTED, BUILD NEW RELATIONSHIPS, LEVERAGE TOOLS, UTILIZE YOUR UPLINE, & again.. GET COMMITTED TO YOUR DREAMS.
If I can do it.... SO CAN YOU!
  Tag Your Leaders
Yea, this is a bathroom selfie. #COMMITTED

Alex Morton
October 21, 2015 •

THANK YOU to everyone who wished me a Happy Birthday today, means the world.

Man, what a year. Honestly what a life thus far. Sitting @ the airport about to take off from NYC over to Europe for a 3.5 week, 10+ country tour. Waking up every single day and doing what I love to do, inspiring others to dream big, believe big, and achieve big. Sounds cheesy, but it's the truth. My passion and life's work is to impact as many people in a positive way as I humanely can. Of course I want to continue to travel the globe, earn millions upon millions of dollars, assist in building the largest network marketing team on the planet, however the way I'll find true significance and fulfillment won't come from money it'll come from helping change other people's lives and leaving the world a better place.

Growing up in a small town I knew I always wanted to do something big. I had a vision of my future burned into my sub conscious mind at a very young age. I didn't know how I was going to do it but it didn't matter because I knew I was going to. Fast forward a few years later I am currently living and have lived "that dream" for almost a half decade & have helped dozens achieve their goals & not just have a life but a lifestyle. I had a measly 3.0 GPA in high school, got rejected from 2/3 college I applied to, got into tons of trouble from 18-21, dropped from the business school, was told I'd never become successful, the list goes on. What's the moral of the story? YOU CAN ACHIEVE YOUR GOALS, PERIOD. NO MATTER WHAT.

Life hasn't always been "sweet" for me. I've had my shares of up and downs, massive struggles in my business, faced with oppositions and tough decisions, however you either win or you learn. You can't go through life with regrets and spending too much time thinking backwards. There's a reason your front wind shield is A LOT bigger than your rear view. Focus on the future and live in the N.O.W. No Opportunity Wasted.

To all my friends and family who genuinely support me I love all of you. To everyone that would love to see me fail, that'll never freaking happen and I appreciate the motivation. To past mentors, thank you for your wisdom. To my current mentors, thank you for your coaching, honesty, inspiration, guidance, and direction. Mom & Dad I love you guys so much. To our incredible team I work, breathe, operate, function, and live for your guy's successes. I'll never freaking stop working and growing to ensure our continued massive victories in this industry for life. I promise you that.

Cheers to the first 25. I've got a good feeling 26 just might be the best year yet...

Dream BIG Dreams & then wake your butt up and chase them every single day until they become your reality!!!
For exact dates, times, venues, private message me
smile emoticon
#ThankYOU
#EuroTour

Alex Morton
October 30, 2015 •

It's crazy when people say things are "unrealistic." I'm like, "Is it more unrealistic than 2 farm boys from Ohio building a steel bird that allows humans to breathe inside of a freaking tube while they're 30,000 feet in the air while it also safely flies them to other cities, states, countries, continents?"

The only things in life that are unrealistic are the ones you label inside your mind unrealistic. Too many people operate out of F.E.A.R. False Evidence Appearing Real. We have nothing to fear but fear itself.

When I was 21 I saw a vehicle that 90% of people thought was an unrealistic way to be able to create time & money freedom at a young age. Glad I didn't listen to the unrealistic thinkers & very happy I didn't quit when times got tough. Most people give up before they even have a chance @ reaching massive success.

Don't let someone who gave up on their dreams tell you that what you want to do is "unrealistic." In fact, if you don't have people telling you that your goals & dreams are too big then you're not dreaming big enough!!!

We're in SWITZERLAND for the next 21 hours, if you're around let's connect!!!
#SwissSwissSwiss

Alex Morton
November 1, 2015 •

When the mind, body, and soul are in a grateful state the universe will conspire to bring you even more to be grateful for. It's also impossible to be angry and grateful at the same time. Everyday when I wake up or right before I shut my eyes I make my "Gratitude List." I sit in silence & think about everything I am grateful for in my life & jot my top 5-10 down.

Today's 10. (Not in order just first to mind)

1. My very honest & open relationship with my parents. (Sometimes too open)
2. A crazy ,nutty ,loving sister & very close relationships with my cousins.
3. Being surrounded by amazing leadership & mentors for business & for life. & having people whom I 100% trust will steer myself & the people I care about most to massive victory.
4. Our incredible team.
5. Healthy Mind.
6. Value adding & mutual beneficial relationships with a select group.
7. Ability to move people emotionally.
8. Doing what I love every moment.
9. Our amazing TEAM.
10. OU Sooners & Dallas Cowboys

I learned the "Gratitude List" activity by one of my mentors Mr. Bob Proctor. Someone who I have studied for years. #GoodnightFromBelgium

Alex Morton
November 24, 2015 •

The difference between successful people and unsuccessful people is that successful people "DO IT." They figure out what they're passionate about and make it their life's work. They set their mind to something & say "I WILL WORK DILIGENTLY IN THE DIRECTION OF MY GOALS AND DREAMS UNTIL THEY COME TO FRUITION." I've come to the realization that life is truly what you make it. When you set your mind to something, draw the line in the sand and tell yourself "I am never going back to the old me," that's where it happens. That's when it clicks. That's when everything changes. Something about the chemistry in your brain changes when YOU DECIDE. You decide what your future will look like, who will be in it, your lifestyle, your homes, cars, money, and most importantly your global impact on changing people's lives.

I'm only 26 years old and I'm well aware I do not know everything. However I do know that 3% of this country and 3% of this world have figured it out on how to achieve massive success. Money isn't everything, your career isn't everything, my career does not define who I am. I find significance within my family, friends, relationships, & making a difference. However I will also be damned if I don't earn 10's of millions of dollars, personally help create dozens of millionaires, & in 10+ years move into the realm of the Jim Rohn, Les Brown, Tony Robbins, Zig Ziglar, AL Williams, Bob Proctor, etc.

I know exactly what my future looks like and I am willing to do whatever it takes to make it happen. DO YOU?
Do you know what you want?

Do you know how to get it?
Are you passionate about your career?
Do you have a 5,10 year plan?
Who are you studying?
Who are you following?
What are your goals and dreams?
What are your daily disciplines?

Bottom line is this. Anything you want in life CAN BE YOURS. No it won't be easy, yes it will suck at times, yes you'll want to give up and quit, yes you'll lose friends, yes you'll have to cut people out, yes you'll have to sacrifice, yes people will call you crazy, yes it will take time, money, energy, effort, grit. & OH HELL YES IT WILL BE WORTH IT.

Look Mama, I made it into FORBES magazine!!!!!!
Chase your dreams. Chase your dreams. Chase your dreams. & never give up!!!

Love Y'all & GO MAKE IT HAPPEN!

Alex Morton added a new video: Alex Morton Mindset.
December 15, 2015 •

YOYOYOYOYOYO about a year ago I created something called Alex Morton Mindset to help share the wealth of knowledge I've accumulated over the last 4 years that has helped me achieve massive success, travel the world several times, help my close friends live their dreams, & end up in The Rolling Stone and Forbes Magazine.

My last 6 months have been INSANE & because of that this project went on the back burner. January 2016 I'm going to be packing your news feed with content that will help you CRUSH IT no matter what your purpose or passion is.

I've been fortunate to have mentors in my life that have truly "been there and done that." Individuals ranging from real estate tycoons, hair salon business owners who do $100,000,000 a year in sales, Multi Millionaires in Network Marketing, & even an individual who is on the Forbes list, owns companies like Patron Tequila, & is a billionaire. I've spent 10's of 1000's of my own money attending seminars learning from people like Les Brown, Tony Robbins, John Maxwell, & dozens of hours with Bob Proctor. That's all cool however it's ALL about RESULTS. If someone doesn't have MASSIVE RESULTS in their life then none of that matters. WIN or GO HOME.
Furthermore, I am a FIRM BELIEVER that achieving success is 98% in between your ears. Aka YOUR MINDSET. I can't teach you math, science, or another language, however I can teach you how to WIN, & WIN BIG. Regardless of your age, race, skin color, economic background, education level, it doesn't matter because when you get your MIND RIGHT everything else GOES RIGHT. Trust Me. I'm going to show you what it actually takes, the grind. The blood, sweat, tears, early mornings, late nights, behind the scenes, everything.

AlexMortonMindset is officially launching in 2016 & I'm going to do everything in my power to help YOU achieve massive freaking success and make it your best year yet. & no I'm not going to charge tons of money for it... The secret to living is giving and this is MY WAY of impacting more people, more often.. & changing even more lives.

At this point in my career I'm no longer solely driven by money. I'm driven by impact and creating a legacy of helping others live their freaking dreams!!!

Make sure we are connected!!

Twitter: @AlexMortonYPR
Instagram: @AlexMortonMindset
Periscope: @AlexMortonYPR
Snapchat: @AlexMortonMindset
Facebook: @AlexMortonMindset
I AM FIRED UP!!!
To YOUR MASSIVE SUCCESS-
Alexander Morton

Alex Morton
December 21, 2015 •

Another incredible tour in the books. I am so proud of all of our leaders in the US markets. Your dedication, commitment, passion, servant driven leadership is what keeps me going, keeps me pushing harder and harder every single day. When you're motivated by your team, you've got to take a second & be grateful for that.

Oregon
Las Vegas
North Carolina
South Carolina
Ohio
Massachusetts
Montreal
Michigan
Illinois

16 nights, 15 flights, slept on couches and floors to 5 star

hotels. Ate ramen noodles to Filets & Lobster. Drove in the car for dozens of hours with leaders going from event to event. Breaking bread, mommas homemade breakfasts, countless dinners. & the best part about going on the road is getting to know the people. That's what it's all about. Hearing their whys, feeling their hearts, seeing their struggles, hardships. The most motivating thing in the world is to see how tough someone has it & then you'll really do whatever it takes to help them win.

I have much respect for internet marketers, keyboard warriors, all of that. But nothing will ever replace human to human, spirit to spirit connection. Sitting down with someone, whether it's a leader or a prospect, & getting to know them. Their story, their family, their purpose in life. I encourage all of the network marketing "leaders" out there to go get in the field, get your hands dirty, dive into the trenches, some of you don't even remember what it's like to do a 2 on 1 because you think you're all high and mighty & you should walk off a plane and into a packed living room, speak, & dip. That's not how this works. Sorry. At least not now, not at this moment.

Go in the field and truly care about your people, team, I call it my family. Like I have said before, it's not about the destination, it's about the journey. Building relationships, getting to know people, caring about them, hearing their stories, & then busting your freaking ass 24/7/365 until you get them across the finish line.

Remember, as you sit around your fireplace, with your beautiful family, in your big home, with your cars, & presents under the tree. There are thousands who can't afford to buy their family what they want for Christmas. Some of those people are on your team. Don't be selfish, be selfless. Go out & help people, change some lives. Remember, giving, feels way better than receiving.

#HappyHolidays

Alex Morton
January 11 •

Crazy to me how people spend so much of their time "hating" on others. Personally, I don't care what other people are doing because I'm focused on what I need to do to grow, evolve, advance, create, elevate, & help the people in my life get to where they deserve to be.

I encourage everyone to spend less time hating, & more time working on your craft, mastering the skills needed for you to win, & love on people. Life's short.

Don't be a hater. Instead be known for your work ethic & your heart for helping others.

Alex Morton
April 15 • Henderson, NV •

99.9% of the time I'm talking about what it takes to become successful, create time and money freedom, live with purpose, impact others, & create an overall abundant and meaningful life.

Today, I want to talk about the things you must stop doing, erase from your mind and habits, & eliminate immediately from your life to avoid ending up a failure.

10 Signs that (if you don't correct yourself) you will end of being a failure:

PS: I use to engage in several of these activities, so don't worry, there's still hope!

1. You love wasting money on STUPID SH*T all the time. ($1K+ nights out, Yeezys, Jordan's, Watches, Cars, Clothes, you can't really afford.)

2. YOU ARE NOT DISCIPLINED.

3. YOU QUIT THINGS TOO EASILY.

4. YOU BLAME OTHERS (Boss, Employees, Team, Parents, Government, Company, Comp Plan, Bf, Gf, etc) FOR YOUR LACK OF SUCCESS.

5. YOU DON'T HAVE UNWAVERING BELIEF IN YOURSELF.

6. YOU CARE WAY TOO MUCH ABOUT HOW OTHER PEOPLE VIEW YOU.

7. YOU DON'T TAKE CARE OF YOUR MIND & BODY WELL ENOUGH.

8. YOU DON'T FIGHT FOR WHAT YOU TRULY WANT OUT OF LIFE, YOU SETTLE.

9. YOU DON'T SET GOALS, INSTEAD YOU JUST GO DAY TO DAY HOPING & PRAYING THINGS GET BETTER.

10. YOU VALUE MONEY OVER PEOPLE & RELATIONSHIPS.

Here's the deal, SUCCESS LEAVES CLUES. I used to struggle with several of the above & still have minor problems with a few. Nobody is perfect. However, we need to do our best in eliminating the things, ideas, habits, thoughts, & actions that don't serve us.

Lets keep pushing towards excellence & striving for greatness!!!
Cheers!

Alex Morton
April 30 at 12:23pm •

We're a part of a generation that's obsessed with looking successful rather than being successful. We've got people with $800/month car payments living in 1 bedroom shacks, girls who spend their last dime on a $3K LV bag as they're making $14/hour, & on weekends in any given club there are groups of the $30,000 a year millionaires "popping bottles."

I partly blame the music, movies, media, however it's mainly "our fault." And what's our fault can also become our solution.

One of my mentors told me to always keep the main thing the main thing. The main thing should be actually becoming successful. Not simply putting a front on to prove how cool you are, impress gold digging bottle rats, or get traction in your business. You know what sells way more than "appearing successful,"... BECOMING SUCCESSFUL BY BEING GENUINE, REAL, HONEST, & HAVING INTEGRITY.

There was once a time where all I cared about was the iced out $60K Rolex & $100K car. Glad I've now graduated from dumb ass thinking school & moved on to focus on inspiring and empowering others. You'll never see a u haul truck behind a hearse so stop chasing stuff & start chasing your passions.

You're already good enough, no need to lie.
#HappySaturday

CPSIA information can be obtained
at www.ICGtesting.com
Printed in the USA
LVOW13*0737300718

585355LV00008B/181/P